Praise for
A Hopeful Earth:
Faith, Science, and the Message of Jesus

"There really is a creation crisis underway, and those of us with a religious bent really are called to stand up for the planet God gave us. This is a powerful and plainspoken book, drawing on the best Wesleyan tradition, to make the case for why we need to take strong action now; read it and act!"

Bill McKibben, American environmentalist, writer, and founder of 350.org

"If you read the Bible, eat regularly, and depend upon water and air for life, you will find this book hopeful and alarming. Alarming because you will discover the certain truth that we are on an unsustainable path and hopeful because we can change our way of living and become good stewards of God's good earth and all of its resources.

The authors lead their readers in non-threatening language to consider the truth of faith and science as they plan their own way of living on this planet. The current reality makes their invitation to live as faithful stewards of the earth very appealing.

Sally Dyck and Sarah Ehrman weave science and faith into a more substantial truth than either can bear alone. A truth that inspires awe and respect for the universe and gives birth to a strong desire to be faithful stewards of this magnificent earth that is home to all living things. It is a resource that families can use for study and reflection and professionals can use in leading small and large groups to take seriously our responsibility to care for the earth."

Rueben P. Job, author of *Three Simple Rules*

"Sally Dyck and Sarah Ehrman articulate a thought-provoking message about Christian stewardship and care for planet earth, a marriage of concepts founded in love, our ever-evolving scientific knowledge, and morality. *A Hopeful Earth: Faith, Science, and the Message of Jesus* will enhance your spiritual life and also stimulate your resolve to 'do good works' in the Wesleyan tradition."

Mark Seeley, Professor of Climatology and Meteorology, University of Minnesota

"Dyck and Ehrman provide a highly useful overview of the dimensions of the current crisis in the created order, punctuated by numerous examples of Christians doing something about it. Informed by scripture, theology, and worship, as well as responsible science and news media, this book could significantly advance both education and action within the church that contribute to the health of the earth."

Ellen F. Davis, Amos Ragan Kearns Distinguished Professor of Bible and Practical Theology, Duke Divinity School

A Hopeful Earth

A Hopeful Earth

Faith, Science, and the Message of Jesus

SALLY DYCK AND
SARAH EHRMAN

ABINGDON PRESS
Nashville

A HOPEFUL EARTH
FAITH, SCIENCE, AND THE MESSAGE OF JESUS

Copyright © 2010 by Abingdon Press

This book is printed on acid-free paper.

Library of Congress Cataloging-in-Publication Data

Dyck, Sally, 1953-
    A hopeful earth : faith, science, and the message of Jesus / Sally Dyck and Sarah Ehrman.
      p. cm.
    Includes bibliographical references (p.   ).
    ISBN 978-1-4267-1037-7 (pbk. : alk. paper)
    1. Human ecology—Religious aspects—United Methodist Church (U.S.)   2. United Methodist Church (U.S.)—Doctrines.   3. Christian life—Methodist authors.   I. Ehrman, Sarah, 1979-   II. Title.
    BX8385.H86D93 2010
    261.8′8—dc22

                                      2010043366

10 11 12 13 14 15 16 17 18 19—10 9 8 7 6 5 4 3 2 1
MANUFACTURED IN THE UNITED STATES OF AMERICA

CONTENTS

Introduction: The Genesis 9

Chapter 1: Our Three Temptations 21

Chapter 2: Consider the Earth 41

Chapter 3: The Love of Stuff .57

Chapter 4: Creating Hell All around Us 73

Chapter 5: Take It to the Water 89

Chapter 6: Bless This Food! .107

Epilogue 133

Notes 135

INTRODUCTION:
The Genesis

The Phone Call: How It All Got Started

"Aunt Sally, Aunt Sally, aren't you a bishop in The United Methodist Church?"

I was working at home one day, and when I picked up the phone, my niece, Sarah, began by asking me this question. I knew this was more of a lead-in than a question and wondered where this conversation was headed.

"Yes, Sarah, I am a bishop in The United Methodist Church."

"Then what is The United Methodist Church doing about the environment?" she demanded.

I gave her what I thought was a fairly convincing argument that The United Methodist Church cares about the environment. I referred to our statements about caring for God's creation and working for social policies on the part of government and industry to reduce pollution and discover new energy sources. I assured her that we even have statements about the compatibility of faith and science. I felt pretty good about all the church says about the natural world and our challenge to care for it. In addition, I mentioned that we were working on several poverty-related issues and on the eradication of malaria as initiatives that are also related to climate change.

"That's all fine, but that's not enough!" Sarah said. "What are you *doing* about the environmental crisis? There is a real environmental crisis going on right now. As I prepare for teaching my high school students, I ready myself for their question to me: 'So what are you *doing* to aid in solving these environmental issues, Miss Ehrman?' Well, I'm teaching them. They are our future and the ones inheriting the world after all.

"But you are a United Methodist bishop. Don't you have far more influence and access to people than a high school teacher or a high school student? So I ask again, what are you *doing*? What is our *church doing*?

"That the church would be leading the charge on this issue seems

9

like a no-brainer to me. The environment is God's creation and so it seems to me that saving it would be top priority for the church. Would it be better if instead of an environmental crisis we called it a *creation* crisis?"

"A creation crisis makes it sound more like a spiritual crisis," I agreed.

"It might not be such a bad thing if it sounds like a spiritual crisis. Answering to God about what happened to God's creation should put most Christians, me included, into a spiritual crisis," she reflected.

There was no dissuading her as her passion bubbled up. Sarah was raised in the church but rarely finds a church that satisfies what she is looking for in a faith community. She has high expectations of the church, based on what she learned from it in her early years, and mostly she is disappointed by us for not "leading the charge" on caring for the environment, eliminating poverty, and making peace.

> "The environment is God's creation. . . . It seems to me that saving it would be top priority for the church. Would it be better if instead of an environmental crisis we called it a *creation* crisis?"

She continued: "I really don't understand how Christians can go on living their lives so completely detached from the environment and continue to be destructive of it. This detachment from and destruction toward the natural world are contradictory to what Jesus taught and the way followers of Jesus are called to live. I feel embarrassed for the church. The church should stand out as a leader on environmental issues.

"There seems to be a lot of thought that goes into 'getting into heaven.' If I were God I'm not sure I'd want the folks who trashed creation to live with me for eternity. Christians should lead the way in sustainability, stewardship, resource management, and species protection. Christians go to church on Sundays but then don't live what they learn. This crisis demands real leadership from people like you and daily living from all Christians in the pews each Sunday."

I injected: "Sarah, I don't know if people really know how to connect their faith and caring for God's creation. It has been made into a political issue or something that certain Sierra Club types get all impassioned about, but not necessarily people of faith. People don't always make the connection between peace and the environment, or poverty and the environment. Maybe people don't know the science that connects the daily choices we make and the impact on the earth over time."

Sarah countered, "The thing is, this isn't the church I remember from my childhood and upbringing. Jesus might not have directly mentioned carbon dioxide emissions, but I remember his lessons being rather direct in terms of how to love and do good. I also remember that Christians claim to use these lessons from Jesus to guide their lives today. I am confused, frustrated, and disappointed that the church is not acting on the values and mission that it claims to represent. I feel like I am coming home to a house different from the one I left. I expect more from the church. Why won't the church speak out and act on these issues, putting faith and practice together?"

"Sarah, it's controversial for many people," I tried to explain.

"Controversial? What's controversial? Are recycling, reducing pollution, preserving ecosystems, and living sustainably controversial? The only controversy I can think of is how these things affect people's pocketbooks and their conveniences and how they call people to change and live differently. Then again, from what I remember, Jesus was also asking people to change and live differently, wasn't he? Like these environmental issues, Jesus' ideas were also a bit controversial and involved to some degree in confronting the powers of his day, weren't they? It seems to get down to how we live: our money, greed, and the immediate benefit of certain individuals. But this shouldn't be at odds with the church. Where do the church's values lie? Maybe the church needs to reassess its values, morals, and big-picture priorities. We fail to look at the big picture, which includes the needs of all people—not just certain ones of us—as well as a long-term perspective. And I think that the bigger picture, the long-term perspective, is more aligned with Jesus' teachings."

"That's interesting," I said. "I'm not sure there is a lot of time spent linking the teachings of Jesus to the care of the environment."

"That ties into what frustrates me about the church," Sarah stated. "People focus on what Jesus says, applying his words to their individual situations and their eternal lives. But I believe that Jesus is talking about community and that he is calling us to apply his words to a different kind of life—a long-term existence here on earth for all creation, for all species, including humanity."

"Then what do we do, Sarah?" I asked.

She answered: "Environmental science needs to be taught in church and explicitly linked to the teachings of Jesus so that people will understand how their faith and the science behind the care of creation are connected."

Over the next couple of months, Sarah continued to call me with some regularity to discuss these connections and to ask questions about the Christian faith and the church's response to God's creation. We decided that we would put together her passion for the care of God's creation and her knowledge of environmental science with my passion for helping the church articulate its faith in a world and culture that aren't making these connections. And so we began work on this book over the course of many months, enjoying our conversations and time together, driving the rest of the family crazy at times, and sharpening my science and her faith. We hope it does the same for readers.

Just a note: both of us wrote this book, but it is written primarily in Sally's voice with Sarah's specific words and thoughts from our discussions noted as coming from her.

Who Are We? What Each of Us Brings to the Conversation

Now for some introductions. We think it will be helpful for you to know something about each of us, and as you go through each chapter, we encourage you to reflect on your own faith and nature stories. What parts of your past and present tie you to the natural world? How do God's creation and your interaction with nature intersect with your faith journey?

Who Am I in This? Sarah Ehrman

I grew up in a small Ohio neighborhood, surrounded by nature. There were few fences, if any at all. The yards gave way to woods that, as a child, seemed endless. My brothers and I were always playing and exploring outdoors. We divided our time among activities such as tackling one another in the name of backyard football, building bridges with logs across small creeks, and poking around for plants we believed to be possible cures for cancer.

Beyond a curiosity for and interest in the natural world, I fell in love with nature, the outdoors, and our planet when I started traveling. The travel bug bit me at the age of fourteen when I went to Australia. Since then I have traveled, often alone, around the world. These trips have allowed me to swim with seals and sea turtles, hike on one of the world's remaining glaciers, play with sticks in flowing lava, stand amid the noise of the rainforest, dive in the Great Barrier Reef, and witness the mysterious remains of a civilization wiped out largely because of environmental collapse. In these and other experiences, I have come face-to-face with our natural world, and every time I am left in speechless awe. What the natural world has to offer, what it is in and of itself, is hard for me to put into words. I only know that it has captured my spirit. I am drawn to it. I am mesmerized by it. I am humbled before it.

Science and the natural world have always fascinated me. How does the human brain store a memory? Why do the leaves turn colors in the fall and not before? What caused the dinosaurs to disappear? Science seems to have the answers to these questions or, as a field of study, is excited about figuring out the answers to the intriguing *how* and *why* questions of our world. Throughout high school and college I focused on physiology and medicine. After college my love for science and desire to travel extensively led me to teach, and it was here that my knowledge and love for environmental science were ignited.

People today, including me, are so busy, so constantly connected to phones and e-mails, working on work, and running the next errand. We feel ultraefficient and connected. But is it possible in all that we are busy doing, and in all the connectedness we feel, that we are not doing what is most important and we are actually distracted from the connection that is the most natural, life-giving, and renewing of all?

When it has been days since I have been outside, sat in the sun, breathed fresh air, or stared at the trees or water or hills, I feel dirty inside, jumbled. I lack a groundedness that I find when I am outside, even for five or ten minutes. The sun, the air, and the sights of the natural world calm my racing mind, renew my tired body, and cleanse my spoiled spirit. My connection to the outdoors feels immediate. Warm sun on my face, a deep breath in, and the sight of green hills turn my disposition 180 degrees. I feel that I can tolerate whatever comes next.

I imagine that this is what it is to be in the presence of God—immediately better, warm, refreshed, and pleasant. Being outside is being in the midst of and experiencing God's creation. Nature, the sun's light, the snow, the green hills, the water in a stream, the grass in our yards, and the fresh air are God. To be too busy or too distracted from time in nature is to have been drawn away from God. And it makes us sick.

I grew up in a family strongly affiliated with The United Methodist Church. We went to church every Sunday, my parents sang in the choir and served on committees, my father was a delegate to the church's annual conference for every year I can remember, and I participated in youth group. Although I never enjoyed Sunday school, I very much enjoyed sitting alone in the back of the balcony of the church during the sermon.

I have always loved a good sermon. That said, I am extremely selective in what I deem a "good sermon." I have no need for fire and brimstone. I despise guilt and shame, "right and wrong," finger pointing and hell warning. On the flip side, I find flowery, praise-filled sermons and most readings and songs to be watery and pointless. I want substance, not a whipping. I want a challenge, not a sentence. I am a major fan of sermons that shed light on a lesson or portion of the Bible in a way that expands my understanding of the text and that pushes me to apply the new knowledge to my life and my work in the world. I want to be educated and challenged. I want to know more, and I want to be and act in ways that are "better"—better for the world, better for people, better for all of God's creation.

Church was just what we did when I was growing up. But despite the expectation of attendance and participation, there was ample space for doubt, reconsideration, questioning, discussion, and a variety of ideas. In high school I attended the adult Sunday school class my dad taught. The class was filled with debate, challenge, and a pushing of new ideas every week. As an eighth grader, with the senior high youth group I led a worship service that with the courage and support of our minister pushed the adults of the congregation to reexamine their perspective on inclusivity as we danced down the aisles to En Vogue's "Free Your Mind." My participation in the church reinforced my critical thinking and reflective skills by creating a space where thinking through God's word and its application in our world was highly encouraged, even expected.

During the church's annual conference, I watched adults in my life debate and define the stances of our church on a variety of issues, from the plight of migrant workers at Florida's tomato farms to the use of Chief Wahoo as the mascot of the Cleveland Indians to the funding of programs to halt the spread of malaria. In this forum, the church went beyond a place to determine what we *believed* to be right and wrong. It became an actor in the making of a better world. It brought to life the beliefs we said we held.

I am frustrated with the faith communities that set up dichotomies where people are scientists *or* they are people of faith; where people pray *or* they care for the earth. For me, there is a natural fit between being a scientist and being a person of faith. This connection has recently been reinforced by my love for and my desire to protect the environment, which I consider not to be the possession of humanity but a gift for each of us to use while we live on earth.

I have been absent from church for many years, but I hold the hope that it can be different. Despite my absence, I have not given up hope that the church and people of faith can have an enormous environmental impact to care for God's creation. From my faith-based upbringing, I believe that we are called to make the world a better place and leave it and its inhabitants better than we found it.

Who Am I in This? Sally Dyck

I grew up on a wheat farm in eastern Washington State. Rolling miles of open land produced mostly grain. It always seemed as if there was an endless horizon around us. When I was a child, we could see Mount Rainier, which was about two hundred miles west, but it has been a long time since the skies have been clear enough to see its prominent beauty.

We lived a long way from anyone else, and my brother, cousins, and I played outside, weather permitting. We would have benefited from modern technology to keep hands, feet, and bodies warm and dry. We poked around the farm, played games, pushed one another on the swing, and roamed freely for hours without supervision.

My mother encouraged an appreciation of nature. Every spring break she took us down to Cow Creek, and we walked along the stream looking at flora and fauna. Years later when my young parishioners took Caribbean cruises and other elaborate spring vacations, I wondered whether in addition to enjoying the entertainment and food they would spend time on deck viewing the water, seeing the sunrises and sunsets, and otherwise appreciating the nature that such a trip could afford.

Church camp was an important part of my growing up. When I was in elementary school, several churches went together to buy property and to develop campgrounds in the Cascade Mountains. The young people loved the place because we had been a part of selecting the property, seeing it developed, and being among the first to spend a few days and nights on it in its original buildings. Hours were spent during the summer, Christmas vacation, and Presidents' Day weekends at the campgrounds. Bones and hearts were occasionally broken over the years, but it was a significant time of being in nature, building community, developing leadership skills, and growing in Christ.

Like Sarah, I enjoyed science in school. By the time I took anthropology in high school and was fairly biblically literate, I began to struggle with science and faith. Part of my compulsion to help address these matters today is that I had no one to answer my questions, listen to my concerns, and work through these issues with me. I roamed our church library for something to read, but nothing was very helpful. I even talked to my science teacher, but he was shocked that such a smart girl like me would even give the creation story a second thought. I knew that wasn't the answer either—at least for me.

When I went to college, I enrolled in a four-year nursing program. Steeped in science, I learned more and more about the intricacies of creation, especially our human bodies. But then I felt a call to ministry and developed a deeper understanding of Scripture. I learned more and more about Genesis and how there are actually two creation stories from different historical contexts.[1] *How could I have not seen that before?* I wondered. I began to see how the Scriptures are truly prescientific. They don't try to answer our questions about how the universe came into being. They answer deeper, timeless questions: Who is God, and who are we in relation to God? Just because we are curious about the origins of the universe does not mean that the Scriptures are able or intended to answer those questions.

My appreciation for nature has increased even more since I started running every morning. I run outside year-round. Even in Minnesota when it's twenty degrees below zero, modern technology has developed outerwear that can keep me from freezing my lungs, fingers, and toes. Any morning's run can easily include not only the beauty of trees, flowers, and other plants, but also creatures such as deer, turtles, possums, raccoons, herons, songbirds, and of course the greatest fear of any runner: skunks. It's a time when I'm aware of God, God's creation, and the beauty of life.

Sarah has provoked me to think more about the connection between faith and science from my present position within the church. It's a critical time for the church to take a lead in addressing the issues and the connections between peace, poverty, and the planet.

The Purpose of the Book:
Our Hope for the Church and Earth

The purpose of this book is to connect our living out the Christian faith with being good stewards of the earth. Much of the biblical and theological undergirding of our contemporary call to care for God's creation focuses on the Hebrew Scriptures; likewise, Jesus' agrarian foundation in life and the Hebrew Scriptures influenced his teachings. In some ways, viewing Jesus as someone with an agrarian economic worldview helps us understand his alternative, even countercultural perspective on the military-industrial complex of his day, what he deemed important, and the persons he found to be important in God's economy of abundance and goodness.

Although Jesus never said anything specific about care for the earth, we do believe that his teachings reflect an ethic of care and a challenge to our ways of living, both encouraging a more faithful response to God and judging us in a culture where we tend to worship power, technology, and domination over others and the earth.

We also want to build a bridge between the scientific world and the faith community. We want to dispel the myth that they are in opposition to each other and that people in one community don't and can't appreciate the other. In fact the two worldviews have more in common than our recent historical differences would cause us to believe at face value. If nothing else, we hope to show that the posture of wonder and amazement is fundamental to being both scientific and faithful people today.

We believe there is hope for the earth when we live the way of Jesus. This book is our attempt to sow a good seed of faith that will be nurtured in the church so that we can appreciate and rejoice in its beauty and hospitality while we are at home on earth as well as leave earth as a home for those who come after us.

Therefore, this book won't provide many practical suggestions about how to make one's personal, home's, or church's carbon footprint smaller, but we hope that readers will utilize the many other excellent resources that describe ways to live more simply and ecologically. We encourage action, not just reflection, in response to our Christian and moral responsibility to care for the earth. But before people start doing things, jumping onboard with the latest fads—some of which aren't environmentally sound—we want people to think deeply about who we are, why we're here on earth, and what our responsibility as followers of Jesus is to creation. We want people to have a bigger picture and more comprehensive idea of the state of the environment. We want readers to reflect deeply on how our mission as a church intersects with our call to care for God's creation.

We desire more than anything else that a commitment to the care of the earth be more than a fad, more than a secular response to a growing moral concern, and so deeply rooted in our Judeo-Christian faith that whether we believe that there is global warming (and we definitely believe there is), whether it's the latest trend (and presently it is, especially with younger people), whether it's convenient (it's definitely countercultural to a desire for convenience), *we choose to care for God's creation because we are followers of Jesus.*

If the church is serious about reaching out to younger generations, the church needs to make the connections between faith and the planet. Sarah is disappointed in the church because she deeply believes that if the followers of Jesus will respond, there is hope for the earth. She believes we can do something and make a difference.

What would Jesus say or do about creation? That has become a constant question for us as we have talked about these concepts and discussed them with other people. Both of us have encountered many people with varying exposure to Christianity who "instinctively" believe that Jesus would want us to care for creation. "Of course Jesus would recycle!" someone said to us over dinner one night as we gathered with some of Sarah's friends, none of whom go to church. Another common response is, "Jesus would be very angry with what we've done with the earth."

If Jesus would care for the earth because it's the right thing to do, then what's holding us back? Wouldn't Jesus want us to do the right thing? By connecting the dots between Jesus and the environment, we hope that this book will challenge your commitment to Jesus and to care for the earth. Without a connection between Jesus and the earth, we believe that good intentions will fall away in caring for the earth and consequently we'll find we're missing out on our commitment to Jesus.

CHAPTER 1
Our Three Temptations

In 1968, when I was a boy, Apollo 8 sent back the first pictures of our planet, that blue-white marble floating in space. Well, those pictures are as out of date as my high school yearbook photo. The planet doesn't look like that or behave like that anymore—there's more blue and less white, more cyclones swirling in the tropics.... It's the image of the beautiful planet in space that we usually carry with us in our mind's eye. And yet that planet is rapidly browning through desertification.

— Bill McKibben [1]

The Laws of Life: Tropical Rainforests

The exact amount of life, even the number of types of living things (species) on this planet is unknown. Estimates range from tens of millions to more than one hundred million species. The tropical rainforests of South America, Southeast Asia, and Africa cover only 2 percent of the earth's surface but are estimated to contain more than half of the world's species. The rainforest supports a vast quantity and diversity of life because the conditions and the forest itself maximize the principle requirements necessary for life. For this reason, the rainforest is a prime example of the natural rules that govern the systems of life in overdrive.

All of life requires energy—energy that ultimately comes from the sun. Rainforests are located on or near the equator, and so they receive a constant twelve-hour supply of sunlight year-round. Trees and other photosynthetic life use the sun's energy to make the chemical food energy for all living things farther up the food chain. When we eat a cow we are indirectly eating the sunlight energy that the grasses the cow ate converted from sunlight energy into chemical food energy.

> The Manu National Park, within a rainforest of Peru, contains 1,300 different species of butterflies, compared to Europe, which has only 320 species. Similarly, the U.S. has about 80 species of frogs while the rainforest-covered island of Madagascar has 300 frog species.[2]

Life also requires water. Rainforests receive between 80 and 430 inches of rainfall per year.[3] At least half of this rainfall is produced by the rainforest trees. A canopy tree in a tropical rainforest will produce 200 gallons of water annually, and an acre of rainforest transpires 20,000 gallons of water into the atmosphere each year.[4] Rainforests make rain!

The sun and warm temperatures combine with the nearly daily heavy rainfall creating constantly high humidity in rainforests. Insects, decomposer fungi, and bacteria thrive in the warm, dark, and moist forest floor and quickly break down any fallen leaves or dead plants and animals back into their nutrient building blocks. These recycled nutrients are taken up quickly and stored in rainforest plant life, as opposed to being stored in soil; thus rainforest soil is nutrient poor.

The diversity of life is the final ingredient or natural law for sustaining a large quantity of life. Species in an ecosystem, and in the world, depend on one another for food, nutrient recycling, shelter, pollination, seed dispersal, protection, and more. They are interdependent, and therefore their lives are woven together into a fabric of sorts. Rainforests are masters of variety and specialized, interdependent relationships.

The enormous canopy trees in rainforests have wide bases (called buttresses) to support their weight, and their tops practically interlock to form a canopy or living roof meters above the forest floor.[5] The plants that manage to survive along the forest floor have huge leaves to soak up the dappled sunlight peeking through holes in the canopy. Vines climb the trees to reach the sun, and once they are at the top they form a walkway-like system for creatures in the canopy.[6] Plants working to access sunlight create multiple layers within the forest. These layers create a variety of places to live and a variety of plant species to eat; thus they support a variety of animal life. With dense vegetation and little wind, plants must rely on insects, bats, and birds to pollinate their flowers and move their seeds.[7]

A single rainforest canopy tree can support thousands of insect species, some of which may be unique to that particular tree.[8] A person can walk hundreds of meters in a rainforest and never see the same species of tree twice.

The combination of the layered forest, the need for pollination, and requirements for decomposition creates a variety of roles for organisms to play. These roles are called "niches." This is not too different from how the word *niche* is used outside of science (for example, "I hope as he travels the world and works in a few jobs that he'll find his niche"). A niche includes where an organism lives, what it eats, what eats it, and how it contributes to the ecosystem. The more niches there are to fill, the more variety in species an ecosystem can sustain.

For example, Brazil nut trees (*Bertholletia excelsa*), large canopy trees found in the Amazon rainforest, depend on the agouti, a small rodent that is the only animal with teeth strong enough to open the grapefruit-sized seedpods. The agouti scatters the seeds across the forest by burying caches far away from the parent tree. For pollination, Brazil nut trees depend on Euglossine orchid bees, the only insects to pollinate the Brazilian nut tree. For this reason, there has been little success growing Brazil nut trees in plantations; they appear to grow only in primary rainforests.[9]

Breaking the Laws of Life

The rainforest's abundance of niches, sunlight, and water, combined with conditions for fast nutrient recycling, explains why rain forests contain half or more of the life on this planet. Unfortunately, when we break these laws by changing these conditions, the abundance of life is destroyed, and in the case of tropical rainforests, humans are unable to restore or rebuild them.

The equivalent of two football fields of rainforest is destroyed every second.[10] That is 120 football fields slashed and burned per minute! At least 40 percent of the tropical rainforests originally on earth have been destroyed, and without significant measures to halt clear-cutting, all forests could be gone by 2050.[11] As we destroy rainforests, we lose access to lifesaving medicines (120 prescription drugs used today are derived from rainforest plants, two-thirds of all plant cancer-fighting compounds come from the rainforest, and the periwinkle of Madagascar increased child leukemia survival rates from 20 to 80 percent),[12] we destroy species that have not even been discovered, we change the formation of clouds and thus the weather system, and we cause countless other unintended consequences. But the main point is that when we destroy rainforests, we break the fundamental laws of life.

Clearing rainforests to plant soybeans, graze cattle, or log trees destroys the strongest, richest fabric of life on this planet and in its place leaves a hot (remember twelve hours of sun 365 days a year), nutrient-poor (remember that rainforest soil is nutrient poor since the nutrients are taken back into trees so quickly), and dry (remember that the rainforest created half or more of the rain that fell) plot of land. To clear a rainforest is to create a desert.

The desert is the opposite of the rainforest. It is still an ecosystem that has a variety of life, but unlike the rainforest that maximizes the requirements of life, the desert has the challenge of making the best of the minimally available principal requirements of life.

The First Temptation:
Salvation Not by Science and Technology Alone

The Holy Spirit led Jesus into the desert, a place with the challenge of life. As Sarah says, if you were going to be stranded somewhere, you'd prefer the rainforest to the desert in terms of the challenge of living. The desert is a desolate and unforgiving environment in which to live. In the Jewish tradition, the desert was a place described as judgment: desolation and destruction.

However, the desert where the Holy Spirit led Jesus is different from our concept of wilderness. Wilderness, like the rainforest, is a place where the environment has continued to flourish with multiple species; the desert is a place where species have been reduced by desolation and destruction. It's a place where there is less life and hope.

> Jesus, full of the Holy Spirit, returned from the Jordan and was led by the Spirit in the wilderness, where for forty days he was tempted by the devil. He ate nothing at all during those days, and when they were over, he was famished. The devil said to him, "If you are the Son of God, command this stone to become a loaf of bread." Jesus answered him, "It is written, 'One does not live by bread alone.'" (Luke 4:1-4)

"*If* you are the Son of God, command this stone to become a loaf of bread" (4:3, emphasis added). As we're relating to what it must feel like to go without food for forty days, we might miss the real temptation. We think the temptation was to make oneself a sandwich and eat, but the devil was more subtle than that!

The test was to challenge Jesus' identity. "*If* you are the Son of God." *If* you really are who you say you are, then do something amazing, perform some magic, and in the process you'll be more popular than sliced bread, the devil seemed to be saying to Jesus. The devil was challenging Jesus to do cheap tricks to prove himself to others. Identity is an ongoing theme in the temptations that we face living on earth. Who are we going to be? The children of God? Or, as we'll discover in chapter 2, consumers?

Jesus performed miracles throughout his ministry, and through seeing or hearing of those miracles, people followed him. But his miracles were motivated by a desire to heal and care for people, not to perform cheap tricks for his own glorification. Turning stones into bread would satisfy his hunger, but it would also override the laws of nature that God had established in creation. We, too, are called to live within the laws of nature in order to find a sustainable lifestyle for ourselves and all the other citizens of this planet. Our first temptation when faced with the desertification and desolation of our planet is to trust in science and technology; surely, they will save us from the effects of what we are doing to God's creation.

Science and technology are the fruit of human endeavor and are disciplines, processes, and tools that we have developed. Through science and technology, for instance, we can find other sources of energy as we near the end of the fossil fuel energy source. Science and technology can help us solve our problems, even the accidents that occur when science and technology fail, but they alone will not pull us out of our predicament. Something else must change within us and change how we live.

Many people may be surprised by the concept that science and technology are compatible with Christian faith. But the first question that we need to address stems from "in the beginning." Is the story of creation in conflict with modern science? We need to consider that question before making our case that we see science and technology as methods to help, and they cannot be our sole salvation.

> **Many people may be surprised by the concept that science and technology are compatible with Christian faith.**

Science and faith are not incompatible when it comes to their understanding of the origins of life. As Sarah often explains to her students, scientists don't know how life started. They have ideas, but no one knows with certainty. Life cannot be made from nonlife, even mimicking supposed conditions on earth billions of years ago. She reminds them that evolution means change, and biological evolution is change in life over time. This is something we can watch in insect populations, observe in the size of human beings over the past thousands of years, and document in fossil comparison. Both science and Scripture know that life began, and now we see life in all its forms is changing.

Sarah says that arguing about the details of evolution while the planet sits in crisis is a misplacement of focus, time, and effort. Her sense of judgment is sharp: "Can you imagine sitting in front of God, finding out that whatever you believed about the origins of life were true, only to have God ask you, 'And so, what did you do to *save* my species, keep my waters and air pure, find renewable energy sources, make peace in nations fighting over resources, and care for the poor among you?"

Genesis 1 is not a "how to create a universe" cookbook; it doesn't answer our question of *how*, but it does answer other questions, such as what our relationship is to God, to other creatures, and to the earth itself. The creation story at the beginning of Genesis (1:1–2:4a) is a beautiful liturgical poem about the home that God made for and gave to us.

Arguing about the details of evolution while the planet sits in crisis is a misplacement of focus, time, and effort.

Carefully reviewing Genesis 1 in terms of the order of creation, we can recognize that it's not meant to describe how creation came into being. What do you see in this ordering of creation? On the first day God created the heavens and the earth and light (1:3-5), but it wasn't until the fourth day that God created the sun and the moon, which give and reflect light on earth (1:14-19). If Genesis 1 were a how-to manual, wouldn't the sun and the moon have been created on the day that light, day, and night were created?

Likewise, on the second day the sky and the sea were created (1:6-8), but it was not until the fifth day that the species that fill the sky and the sea were created: birds and fish (1:20-23). On the third day earth's dry land, its vegetation, and the definition of the sea were formed (1:9-13), but it was not until the sixth day that the dry land was filled with animals, humanity, and vegetation for food (1:24-31).

Instead of giving a how-to approach to the story of creation, the ordering of creation in Genesis is a mnemonic device by ancient storytellers so they could remember the way to tell this beautiful story and thereby keep the telling of it consistent over time. Eventually the story was written down. Its beauty and message are in the proclamation and affirmation that God created all; it is God's creation, and God established the laws of nature as part of that existing order.

Out of Faith Came Science

People of faith began to develop the field of science. It's hard for our modern minds to understand the role that Christianity played in bringing about the development of science.

"What?" you may be asking. "I thought science and faith were always at odds with each other!"

We forget that science and faith haven't always been at odds with each other. That's a relatively recent phenomenon, spanning mostly the twentieth century. The history of science and Christianity is a complex relationship, but it has not always been one of conflict. In fact, the Christian faith actually encouraged scientific observation, exploration, and experimentation.

David A. Wilkinson has a PhD in theoretical astrophysics. At least that was his first career. But then he became a British Methodist clergyperson. He writes that our Judeo-Christian faith encouraged science because the universe was created by God, and as humans we can never figure it out solely with our minds. We need to observe it, ponder it, explore it, and experiment with it in order to better understand it.

Wilkinson also argues that since God created humanity in God's own image, our fundamental belief is that we can also come to understand these laws of nature as we observe them, record them, analyze them, and build on them over the ages. This is the result of a miraculous mind that God created and that is able to become sophisticated in methods of observation.

Therefore, the Judeo-Christian tradition provided the impetus for the gift of the scientific model of humanity.[13] Science and technology aren't in opposition to our faith, but we're still to avoid insisting that science and technology should save us from our ecological sins.

What Will Save Us?

One temptation is to believe that science and technology will save us. I know people who think that they can eat and live however they want because by the time the effects of their habits influence their health, there will be a pill or a treatment to change their lifestyle outcomes. Too often we have had this perspective on the creation crisis: science and technology will take care of any accidents or the overall negative impact of our living. As the oil crisis in the Gulf of Mexico occurred in the spring of 2010, Tina Carter, a United Methodist clergywoman who also holds a PhD in chemistry, commented on this very point:

> We have created an idol of science. We need to get back
> to worshipping God. We need to quit seeing environ-

mental disasters happen and pointing our fingers at those who are "godlike" enough to solve our issues—forgetting that every time we point one finger, there are four fingers pointing back at ourselves.

As a scientist, I can't help but think that we need to slow down—slow down our consumption, our demand, our desire for instant results.[14]

We can't make science our idol; we can't just trust science and technology to save us from the ecological mess we're in because of who we are: followers of Jesus. Will we make the lifestyle changes of which Jesus spoke in order to restore some semblance of health to this earth, God's creation? Or will we be tempted to trust solely in science and technology to bail us out?

Jesus responded to the devil by saying that "one does not live by bread alone." Jesus' first temptation was to defy the laws of nature and turn stones into bread. Later he also refused to defy the laws of nature to save his physical life. We can't rely on science and technology to restore and rebuild the earth when we have destroyed it, as we have done with the devastation of the rainforest. We, too, must refuse to defy the laws of nature embodied in science and technology, thinking that they will save us from our pride, greed, and failure to remember who we are—followers of Jesus.

The Second Temptation:
Salvation Not by Politics and Economics Alone

But the devil wasn't finished with Jesus yet!

Then the devil led him up and showed him in an instant all the kingdoms of the world. And the devil said to him, "To you I will give their glory and all this authority; for it has been given over to me, and I give it to anyone I please. If you, then, will worship me, it will all be yours." Jesus answered him, "It is written, 'Worship the Lord your God, and serve only him.' " (Luke 4:5-8)

What kind of power would Jesus use in his life and ministry? The devil offered Jesus the opportunity to rely on politics and economics.

> God blessed them, and God said to them, "Be fruitful and multiply, and fill the earth and subdue it; and have dominion over the fish of the sea and over the birds of the air and over every living thing that moves upon the earth." (Genesis 1:28)

Jesus resisted the temptation to rely on politics and economics alone to solve the problems of the world throughout the ages. He reverses an interpretation on the biblical concept of *dominion* when it comes to our ecological crisis.

The first question that many people ask about care of creation goes all the way back to the Garden of Eden when God gave humanity dominion over creation:

> Then God said, "Let us make humankind in our image, according to our likeness; and let them have dominion over the fish of the sea, and over the birds of the air, and over the cattle, and over all the wild animals of the earth, and over every creeping thing that creeps upon the earth."...God blessed them, and God said to them, "Be fruitful and multiply, and fill the earth and subdue it; and have dominion over the fish of the sea and over the birds of the air and over every living thing that moves upon the earth." (Genesis 1:26, 28)

The second temptation for us today is to believe that we as human beings are the pinnacle of creation and thereby have dominion over it to do with it what we will. What does it mean that God gave humanity dominion over the earth and commands humanity to subdue it?

Biblical scholar Ellen Davis describes dominion as "mastery among" the creatures.[15] Mastery is the expertise that humanity has to be the steward of creation. Mastery *among* is different than over! Those tricky prepositions make a big difference! Mastery *among* describes the interconnectedness or interdependence that all of God's creations, including humanity, have with each other.

To have dominion means that humanity cares for the land in such a way that its occupants are able to fulfill the rest of the commandment: to be fruitful and multiply. If humanity treats the earth and its creatures in such a way that the land is unable to sustain life, then humanity has failed in its commandment to have dominion, care, and stewardship over creation. This is a major consequence or test to what dominion is whether the land and its species, including humanity, be able to be "fruitful and multiply." God provided in the Law sustainable practices that would provide for its well being, such as a Sabbath year when the earth is allowed to re-nourish itself by being left fallow (Leviticus 25:1-7).[16]

Usufruct is a word that comes from "Roman and Civil Law," putting together use (*usus*) and enjoyment (*fructus*—which is the root word of fruit) to mean "the right of using and enjoying all the advantages and profits of the property of another *without altering or damaging the substance*"[17] (emphasis added). To exercise dominion is to use what has been given to us without damaging it or altering it in ways that no longer provide for life and life abundant for all on earth.

> **Biblical scholar Ellen Davis describes dominion as "mastery among" the creatures. Mastery *among* is different from *over*! Those tricky prepositions make a big difference. Mastery *among* describes the interconnectedness or interdependence of all of God's creations, including humanity.**

Back to *identity* in these temptations. Our living in the "image of God" and caring for the earth are intimately connected. Davis translates Genesis 1:26 as follows: "Let us make humankind as our image, after our likeness; *that* they may exercise mastery among the fish of the sea, etc."[18] Note that Genesis 1:26 makes it clear that the "conformity to the image of God is the single enabling condition for the exercise of 'mastery' among the creatures."[19]

If we are living in the image of God, we will be good stewards of the power and resources that we have been given by God. Dominion is a divinely commissioned relationship with God, earth, and humanity. When Jesus refused the devil's offer of political and economic power, Jesus was living out true dominion in his right relationship with God.

As followers of Jesus today, we need to participate in and influence the political powers to care for the earth. But whether we are politically Left or Right or somewhere in between, we cannot rely solely on the political and economic systems of our day to solve the problems related to the care of God's creation. The political and economic systems of our day actually work *against* some of the major changes that would demonstrate true dominion of the earth so that it can "be fruitful and multiply."

Usufruct is a word that comes from Roman and civil law, putting together use (*usus*) and enjoyment (*fructus,* which is the root word of fruit) to mean "the right of using and enjoying all the advantages and profits of the property of another *without altering or damaging the substance"* (emphasis added). To exercise dominion is to use what has been given to us without damaging it or altering it in ways that no longer provide for life and life abundant for all on earth.

The connections between politics and economics are revealed in our continued dependence on fossil fuels when science warns us about it. The lack of regulations for the automotive industry has prevented the development and the acceptance of more fuel-efficient vehicles. Our agricultural practices have sacrificed quality of food (as we dump pesticides on our plants and pump antibiotics into our animals) and a living for many farmers for the sake of quantity (without regard to the quality of the soil) and the wealth of a few farmers in our country. Again, science keeps telling us that more and smaller farms will better feed our nation and provide food safety.

While making some of the innovative shifts toward environmentally friendly automobiles, energy sources, and food production may actually generate a variety of new jobs and industries, politics and economics often work against these changes as we look at each natural resource in this book, the conflict between politics and economics (dominion and power over the earth instead of care of the earth without unduly damaging it) becomes apparent; we can't rely on politics and economics to save us from what we have done to the earth and the effects that are already causing distress for many people around the world, including the United States.

Jesus' response to the devil's temptation to sell his soul to the political powers of his day was to say, "Worship the Lord your God, and serve only him." But where are we putting our trust? Just as we can use science and technology but can't trust in them alone, we can influence politics/government and economy/business to help but can't trust that they will solve our ecological predicament.

Ultimately the power of the human spirit changes things. We need what Jesus himself realized as the only power, strategy, and commitment that can outdo the "powers and principalities" of this earth: the power of the cross as exemplified in limiting our consumption, practicing lifestyles that reflect Jesus' values and that have as a result an earth for our children and for generations to come.

The Third Temptation:
Not Saved by *Personal* Salvation Alone

The devil still wasn't finished with Jesus, and the most critical temptation was yet to come: expecting God to rescue him:

> Then the devil took him to Jerusalem, and placed him on the pinnacle of the temple, saying to him, "If you are the Son of God, throw yourself down from here, for it is written, 'He will command his angels concerning you, to protect you,' and 'On their hands they will bear you up, so that you will not dash your foot against a stone.'" (Luke 4:9-11)

It was no accident that the devil took Jesus to the highest and the most sacred place—to the pinnacle of the temple. Jesus had just come from the high religious moment of his baptism. In the third temptation the devil wanted Jesus to exploit his relationship with God to his advantage.

Our temptation today is to believe that God will magically save us from our own destruction, just in time for us to be swooped away from the burning inferno that we have created through our unsustainable living. Surely God won't let us suffer on this planet.

Whenever Sarah teaches about the environment, she tries to emphasize that these aren't things that people in the far-off future will have to deal with. We are dealing with them now, and her students will definitely have to address them in their lives. To stimulate their imaginations, she asks her students to imagine that when they read books about tigers, bears, and elephants to their grandchildren, it is entirely likely that one or all of those animals will no longer exist or exist only in zoos. How will they answer when their grandchildren ask what happened to these animals?

That hooks them, and she gives statistics about the depletion of natural resources and overconsumption. "What would happen if there weren't enough resources to feed the population?" she asks them. "What if we had a potluck in our classroom that could feed only ten, but there were thirty of us?" They know the answer to that question pretty quickly: "Fighting would break out!" Lack of resources results in violence whether it's in a classroom of students using their imaginations or on a planet with people facing the reality of scarce resources.

Often during these exchanges, students remark that they aren't worried. They feel confident that in a "fight" for resources they will come out ahead. Others aren't worried because, as one student piped up, "God is going to come down and save me because it will be the end of the world." God has planned for the end of the world, and those who are "good" Christians will be "swooped up" and taken out of all the environmental destruction.

The first time Sarah heard this response she was stunned. Then she heard it in class after class, year after year. "Good" religious people are teaching that God will save them from our exploitation of resources and destruction of the earth as well as the poverty and violence connected to these practices.

Sarah tries a little reality therapy by asking, "Why would God step in and save you when God hasn't stepped in for the billion people who currently lack access to drinkable water and adequate food and who live and work in garbage dumps for pennies a day in order to survive?" That stops them for a moment as they ponder whether God's role really is to save us from ourselves or whether we're meant to live in such a way that life can be sustained on the earth for our benefit here and now as well as other places and in the future.

Some are tempted to stay in a high and spiritual place, piously expecting that God will save us, and they refuse to become a part of the solution. These people regard caring for God's creation as a non-religious, nonspiritual matter. It's something that "tree huggers and hippies," or creation-worshiping people or fanatics—not serious Christians—do. If our only spiritual solution to the environment is to throw ourselves off the highest pinnacle, expecting God to save us from ourselves, we're in trouble!

Renewing God's creation is part of the social holiness that John Wesley, founder of Methodism, challenged us to live:

> The Gospel of Christ knows no religion but social, no holiness but social holiness. You cannot be holy except as you are engaged in making the world a better place. You do not become holy by keeping yourself pure and clean from the world but by plunging into ministry on behalf of the world's hurting ones.[20]

Too many of "the world's hurting ones" aren't visible and real to those who can make a difference. A "social concern" is a disembodied statistic or concept rather than a child of God. For instance, slavery continued to exist in this country because "the world's hurting ones" didn't matter as much as others' economic or political way of life. The matter of caring for God's creation is a spiritual crisis and demands all of us to engage in "making the world a better place." And we will get our hands dirty as we dig in the earth to grow more of our food, and our brows will get sweaty as we walk more and drive less.

Jesus' response to the devil was: "Don't test the Lord your God." Are

Are we testing God's patience with our unsustainable living and the way in which we make our faith so private and personal instead of putting our faith into action, our words into deeds, and our devotion into sacrifice for the future and for others?

we testing God's patience with our unsustainable living and the way in which we make our faith so private and personal instead of putting our faith into action, our words into deeds, and our devotion into sacrifice for the future and for others? "When the devil had finished every test, he departed fro him until an opportune time" (Luke 4:13).

Perhaps there's a fourth temptation. As we were approaching the publication of this book, the news reports about the crisis in the Gulf of Mexico were that the well was capped, the oil was no longer gushing into the waters, the high temperature in the Gulf was dissipating the oil, and the commercial fishers were going back out on their boats. The scope of disaster, even in these crises, and the urgency of making changes to prevent something similar from happening were waning. "We got through this one and we'll get through the next without having to change anything that we do or how we live" seems to be the prevailing spirit. The next time might not be so "opportune" for us.

As followers of Jesus, we need to follow him and resist all four of these temptations in order to make a difference in the world, beginning with our own lives.

An Inspiring Example

Wangari Maathai is a modern-day prophet in the desert of Kenya. A biologist by training, she became the first woman in central Africa to earn a PhD and was the surprise winner of the 2004 Nobel Peace Prize. Her work demonstrates the connection between the effects of the environment and peace.

She remembers when she was a little girl that her mother would send her out to collect wood for the fire, just like all the other girls did. But her mother's instructions always included the admonition that she was not to collect wood from a strangler fig tree. When she asked her mother why, her mother said that this "is a tree of God. We don't cut it. We don't burn it. We don't use it. They live for as long as they can, and they fall on their own when they are too old."[21] Although her mother may not have fully understood the biological truth of the concept of a holy tree, the tree provided for the sustainability of the land and protected people from desertification, landslides, and other natural disasters.

Maathai left Kenya to go to a university in the United States in 1960 and returned five and a half years later. When she returned, her biological research sent her out into the countryside to collect parasitic ticks from cow ears to study. When she went, she observed the landscape around her. She saw soil erosion that also blocked roads. The cows were sickly and skinny because there wasn't much vegetation for them to eat. The people's health didn't look much better than that of the cows. Deforestation of indigenous lands had occurred so that tea and coffee could be grown for export. Likewise, other cash crops were grown instead of the traditional crops that fed the people. Families were eating more and more processed foods, which were low in nutrients, because there was less firewood available for cooking. Slowly people's diets changed for the worse. Mostly people accepted that this was the way things were; this was progress. If they wanted to better themselves, they believed, they needed to cut down the trees, plant cash crops, and never mind that not only the cows but also the children and everyone else were starving.

Maathai was one of very few female professors at the University of Nairobi, and the women academics were treated very poorly and denied the rights of the male professors. These injustices against her as a woman professor were disturbing to her, so when she was scheduled to attend the first United Nations Women's Conference in Mexico in 1975, she was determined to set the agenda to focus on the discrimination against women in academics. She went to the first meeting intent upon her goal, but she came away with quite a different agenda,which set the course of her life ever since. At the meeting she heard about the rural women's lives, asking for more and better food, for firewood, for help out of poverty. The women came from the highlands where she grew up, and "it struck me that in that period of less than 10 years, so much change had taken place in the environment."[22]

She decided to organize the women to plant trees. Trees would bring back what had been lost by the deforestation, devegetation, desertification, and desolation that threatened the livelihood of the people who lived there, much less the rest of the species. "The earth was naked," she said. "For me, the mission was to try to cover it with green."[23] She organized what became the Green Belt Movement in 1977, mobilizing an effort of women and men to reclaim the land and its resources, and by so doing, she empowered others.

The Green Belt Movement with Maathai at its helm planted not only trees but also ideas.[24] Powers and principalities did not applaud her efforts. Instead she met fierce resistance from those who didn't want the movement to survive, including the government itself. As a result of her efforts, she was ridiculed, beaten, and put in prison to keep her from her goals.

The temptation was to receive acclaim for herself as an academic, but she remembered who she was and resisted the temptation to satisfy her own desire and instead mobilized and empowered people to reclaim their land and livelihood.

The devil's work is never done. The journey continues into our own lives as we seek to follow Jesus.

Continuing the Journey—Do No Harm

In 2007, author and bishop Rueben Job resurrected and updated the language of the three simple rules that John Wesley taught the early Methodists:

Do no harm.
Do good.
Stay in love with God.[25]

Since then, countless Christians have turned to these simple rules to guide them in their daily living, just as John Wesley intended and also as Bishop Job had hoped. The context in which Job reflected on the three simple rules was "the world in which we live."[26] What directs us in our choices and guides our decisions? We have become so divided and divisive after an earlier generation has worked for a "world of peace and plenty for all"[27] and there is disappointment that

nations are increasingly hostile toward one another, communities are divided around issues of education, development, and the status quo. Religion is divided with each claiming to have a firm grip on the truth. Denominations and congregations are divided over doctrine and what constitutes faithful discipleship and mortal sin. And families are divided by competing agendas, rival priorities, and the daily pressure to survive and thrive in an increasingly competitive culture.[28]

As a result, nations, communities, religions, denominations, congregations, and families are weakened by this divisiveness and strife, Job sadly states. Being Christian doesn't appear to be much different from being someone without a religious commitment. Surely there is a way of living that reflects our best, most Christlike selves in the midst of a complicated, divisive, complex, and confusing world, especially when it comes to living sustainably.

In his reflections on the three simple rules, Job focuses primarily on the ways in which we relate to other people: "in ways that are healing and life-giving, not destructive and life-denying."[29] Like Wesley, he encourages and challenges Christians to attend to these simple rules as a guide for Christian living in our relationships with others and with God, based on the Great Commandment (to love God) and the second commandment (to love our neighbor as ourselves).

In light of our Christian faith and God's creation, I think the three simple rules provide guidance in a slightly different but helpful way. They give us guidance in taking the next step in our lives when all the choices and information are so complicated and confusing at times that it's hard to know what the next, best step is for us and for our communities, churches, and nations to take in living more sustainably.

A Commitment

Look at the ways that you unintentionally harm your community and the planet. What are steps you can take to change this trend in your life?

CHAPTER 2
Consider the Earth

More science and more technology are not going to get us out of the present ecologic crisis until we find a new religion, or rethink our old one.

— **Lynn White** [1]

Living in God's House

What if there was a man who spent years building a beautiful and structurally sound home? The roof and walls protected the house from the elements, and the foundation was solid, even against an earthquake.

Inside the home, he put a lot of care into choosing the floor coverings, curtains, appliances, furniture, and art. Everything was to be functional as well as beautiful. Simplicity was the standard of beauty. Windows let in a lot of light. The house was powered by solar energy.

The man put as much care into the surrounding gardens as he did into the house. There were gardens of flowers, vegetables, and fruit trees—everything good to eat. He even installed a swimming pool for the enjoyment of those who came to visit him.

When the house was finished, the man decided to ask his son to watch over it while he went away for a while. He encouraged his son to use it fully, enjoying himself and offering it as a gift to others. He told his son to eat from the gardens, swim in the pool, and "make yourself at home because it is yours for as long as you'd like."

The son enjoyed the house and all that it offered him. He invited his friends over and they enjoyed it too, but they weren't very careful about the way they treated the gardens, the swimming pool, and even the house itself. They left food and papers around, and the garbage began to pile up, smelling and looking terrible. There were holes in the walls, the results of punches thrown by people who had gotten into fights. All the furnishings were filthy, torn, or smelly because the son didn't take care of them and his friends kept misusing them.

The son let the garden get overgrown with weeds because tending it was inconvenient. He never cleaned out the pool and algae grew all over it, so no one wanted to swim in it anymore.

The son hadn't invested in its upkeep. The utilities were shut off, and the bills were in the hundreds of thousands of dollars. How would he ever be able to catch up on the expenses of repairing and restoring the house when he couldn't afford to care for it in its current condition?

Then the father came home—and saw his beautiful house totally ruined.

What if you were the son to whom the house was entrusted? How would you ever face your father? What would you say to him? Would you blame others who damaged it? Would you say that you got into tough times and couldn't adequately care for it? Or that you were so busy at work that the garden and pool got away from you? And, well, you got behind on the utility bills, but what were you supposed to do, freeze?

The beautiful house is a disaster! The relationship between the father and son is a disaster!

We are living this parable as we live on earth today. The origin of the English word *ecology* comes from the Greek *oikos*, which means "house." This planet is our house, the home we have to live on, entrusted to us by God. When we contemplate what we've done to God's home, how do we face God, the Creator of our home? What do we say in our defense? What does it mean to be a follower of Jesus when we have trashed our home, God's earth?

The State of Life: HIPPO—The Sixth Extinction

What is the human niche? What is our role on this planet? Are we given the earth to pillage as we please? Are we given a responsibility to be thoughtful stewards of the earth, using the natural goods and services freely provided, but as a part of the earth and with an interest in the planet and the rest of life equal to our interest in ourselves? It may even be worth asking whether we think our role is the pinnacle or the steward and whether saving the planet is simultaneously in the best interest of humans as well.

We are currently in the midst of the sixth mass extinction. The last mass extinction involved the loss of the dinosaurs and roughly 30 percent of species on earth. Extinction is natural, but the current extinction rate is between one hundred and one thousand times the natural extinction rate. Scientists say that at the rate we are going, we could lose up to 50 percent of species on earth by 2050. This is not a difficult statistic to believe when one considers the number of species in the tropical rainforests and the rate at which the rainforests are being destroyed.

Scientists say that at the rate we are going, we could lose up to 50 percent of species on earth by 2050.

To better understand this massive assault on life, one must consider HIPPO: Habitat destruction, Invasive species, Pollution, (over)Population, and Overconsumption (or overuse) of resources. Each of these five factors contributes to the enormous loss of species we face today.

H: A perfect example of habitat destruction is the melting of the Arctic tundra, which has put polar bears and other species at great risk because they are unable to adapt quickly enough to climactic changes. Coral reefs around the world are bleached or die as the oceans warm. Rainforests, grasslands, and prairies are being converted to farmland. Marshlands are drained for building homes or growing crops. The loss or alteration of ecosystems on earth changes the quantity and diversity of life that the planet can support.

I: Invasive species are not native to an area but have been moved there. Invasive species usually lack natural predators and therefore reproduce at an unchecked rate. They also tend to be generalist species that are not as particular about what they eat and scavenge. As their numbers grow, they outcompete the native species of plants or animals, disrupting the interdependent relationships created over centuries or millennia, and often cost humans millions of dollars. The zebra mussel of the Great Lakes is a prime example of an invasive species.

P: Pollution puts species at risk on almost every front. Air pollution settles into water and the chemicals work their way up the food chain, affecting life all along the way. For instance, when we burn coal, mercury is released into the air. When the mercury settles, a large amount settles into the oceans, is ingested by microscopic plankton, and works its way up the food chain into the muscles of cold-water fish. This is why eating tuna, even a couple of cans a week, increases human blood mercury levels near the toxic level. Air-, water-, and land-related pollution drastically harms life on this planet.

P: Large population numbers, the human population in particular, tax life in a variety of ways. As the number of humans on this planet grows, and as the humans continue to live at higher and higher standards, more space is required for building homes and for growing food. Water, energy, mineral resources, and the other goods and services of the earth are demanded at ever-increasing rates. People on earth require an astounding amount of resources and then produce an equally astounding amount of waste from using those resources.

O: Our overconsumption, harvesting, and use of the planet are destroying life on earth. We use rivers by building dams. We use the wood in trees for paper, hardwood floors, and building materials. We poach exotic species to be sold at exorbitant prices as displays of our wealth and status. We use, harvest, and consume life at ever-increasing rates.

It is not going well with life. Every letter of HIPPO appears as a disaster for the natural world, but what can we do? The key to saving the life on this planet, including our own, is focusing on biodiversity. Biodiversity is a variety in living things, and it is our safety net in an uncertain world. Genetic biodiversity, the variation in the genes within a species, provides security that as changes in the environment occur, some individuals within the species will survive. Species diversity, the variety of different kinds of life in an area, provides stability to the ecosystem (such as the high degree of interdependence and the rich fabric of the rainforest ecosystem) and provides an increase in available niches. The fact that species occupy and create niches and that species rely on one another for food, shelter, pollination, or protection is the interconnection, the fabric of life on this planet. Removing species from the fabric of life eventually leads to the unraveling of ecosystems. And to lose ecosystems, through species loss or outright destruction such as rainforest clearing and coral reef bleaching, is to lose the very places on this earth that purify our water, cleanse our air, make our oxygen, grow our food, provide our medicines,[2] regulate our climate, and do so much more.

It is estimated that the goods and services that nature provides free of charge would total at least $33.2 trillion.[3] Beyond the dollar value that we can put on nature, the medicines and materials that it provides us, or even that we are a part of the fabric of which we are destroying, the ecosystems of this planet are more beautiful than can be described in words. Nature is gorgeous beyond explanation—seeing it leaves one in awe. To destroy something so beautiful, quite possibly the artwork of God, seems counter to Christian values.

> It is estimated that the goods and services that nature provides free of charge would total at least $33.2 trillion.

When we contemplate what we've done to God's home, how do we face God, the Creator of our home? What do we say in our defense? What does it mean to be a follower of Jesus when we have trashed God's earth?

Consider the Earth—Jesus Did!

Jesus directed his disciples' attention to creation around them in order to teach them how to live as his followers, and he continues to direct our attention to nature around us.

> He said to his disciples, "Therefore I tell you, do not worry about your life, what you will eat, or about your body, what you will wear. For life is more than food,

and the body more than clothing. Consider the ravens: they neither sow nor reap, they have neither storehouse nor barn, and yet God feeds them. Of how much more value are you than the birds! And can any of you by worrying add a single hour to your span of life? If then you are not able to do so small a thing as that, why do you worry about the rest? Consider the lilies, how they grow: they neither toil nor spin; yet I tell you, even Solomon in all his glory was not clothed like one of these. But if God so clothes the grass of the field, which is alive today and tomorrow is thrown into the oven, how much more will he clothe you—you of little faith! And do not keep striving for what you are to eat and what you are to drink, and do not keep worrying. For it is the nations of the world that strive after all these things, and your Father knows that you need them. Instead, strive for his kingdom, and these things will be given to you as well.... For where your treasure is, there your heart will be also." (Luke 12:22-31, 34)

Jesus tells his followers to consider the ravens, to notice the lilies. Consider *creation*—Jesus did. Jesus' perspective on healthy spiritual living is more connected to his agrarian worldview than most of us in our nonagrarian worldview can appreciate. His perspective is deeply rooted biblically and culturally in his Hebrew Scriptures and tradition. It's nearly impossible for us as American Christians to appreciate the depth of importance that land—the earth itself—has played in our Judeo-Christian Scriptures and its impact on Jesus himself, ecause most of us lack an agrarian worldview.

> **Then Jesus said to his disciples: "Therefore I tell you, do not worry about your life. . . . Consider the lilies, how they grow."**
> **(Luke 12:22, 27)**

Jesus' agrarian worldview is evidenced in the agricultural stories, such as the planting of seeds (Mark 4:1-20), pointing to a fig tree in its greening season (Mark 13:28), or forecasting weather (Matthew 16:2-3; 24:27). These and other passages reveal Jesus' agrarian world-view, which shaped his alternative sense of economics—God's economics of abundance instead of our economics of scarcity. His messages are counter to the empire's definitions of power. His value of community is evidenced in his outreach to the least, lost, and left out of the economics of Rome, mostly people in captivity or poverty. It's much less individualistic than ours. An agrarian worldview lives within limitations and restrictions for the purpose of providing for the common good for generations to come; more, bigger, and better are not the values of agrarianism in the first century or the twenty-first.

Jesus came out of the Jewish tradition that did "natural theology," seeing in nature a way to describe symbolically and metaphorically that which can't easily be seen or put into words, such as who God is, what God's relationship is with us, and how God wants us to live on earth. The problem for most Americans is that we have become disconnected from nature/creation, and the result is disastrous!

Disaster Waiting to Happen

The origin of the English word *disaster* literally means *dis*, or "separation," and *aster*, or "star." Disaster is to be separated from the stars. In its nautical origins, to be separated from the stars for very long out on the open seas would be a disaster, causing one to lose one's bearings and get lost. When we're disconnected from nature, we too are headed for disaster because as a result we're increasingly disconnected from God, others, and a respect and reverence for God's house.

When we're separated from nature physically and spiritually, we're in danger of losing an important aspect of what it means to be human: a capacity for wonder. When we lose our capacity for wonder at the ordinary things around us, such as our bodies, the miracle of the intricacies of nature, and even the atrocities that humankind has inflicted on nature, we lose respect and reverence for ourselves, others, and God. Abraham Joshua Heschel emphasized throughout his writings that awe precedes faith. When our sense of awe and wonder diminishes, we begin to make ourselves, instead of God, the center of the universe; that is the very definition of sin.

Poet Brendan Kennelly describes the way that our lives are impoverished and spiritually endangered in his poem that begins with the line, "Hell is the familiar all stripped of wonder."[4] For many of us, creation has been "stripped of wonder." Kennelly recognizes what the Hebrew and Christian Scriptures have taught us throughout the ages: "When wonder died in me power was born."[5] The power that is born is the sense that we are the center of the universe.

Science and faith share a profound basic dimension for their development in the experience of mystery and wonder. Over the years Sarah has taught all sorts of life sciences, including medical science, anatomy and physiology, biology, and of course environmental science. Once a student said, "Miss Ehrman, whenever you talk about any system in the body or ecological system, you talk about it like it's really a *miracle* or something."

What is a miracle? One person can look into another's eye and see something beautiful or ordinary; it can be "stripped of wonder," or it can be literally "a miracle or something." As a scientist, Sarah feels a sense of awe, wonder, and amazement. Evolutionary biologists have difficulty explaining how such a system as the human eye came into existence through the accepted evolutionary principles. The intricacies of the inner workings of the human eyeball are something at which to marvel, to wonder about, to consider as something truly miraculous. The more a scientist knows, the more the scientist knows how little is known! Likewise, the more we consider the ways of God, the more we realize how little we know about the mystery and wonder that is God.

Remembering Who We Are—Followers of Jesus

Jesus tells his disciples, "Don't worry about what you eat or wear." Doesn't Jesus care about what we eat or wear? If I were hungry or naked, I think I would have some objection to an apparent lack of concern for my basic human needs. But we have no indication that Jesus' disciples ever went without food or clothing. Furthermore, Jesus always cared about people's basic human needs, as he provided for them when they were hungry after days of listening to his teaching on the hillsides. He fed the thousands again and again (Matthew 14:13-20; 15:32-38).

Sarah and I love to cook and eat healthy food together. It was a regular ritual in the writing of this book. We also have been known for spending more money than we should on clothing (me more than

Sarah!). Jesus' instruction not to worry about food or clothing was meant for people such as Sarah and me, who do not go without the basic necessities of life but can sometimes get confused about our identity, our needs, and our ability to change.

Just as Jesus' temptations were challenges to his identity, so we face temptations about our identity. We have become consumers, and being consumers converts us to another religion. As Sarah says, it seems that many people's religion has become consumerism, doing whatever they must to maintain a style of living, even sacrificing in order to make more money to acquire more things. As she looks around, she sees most people, including religious people, ascribing supreme importance to the size of their houses or what's inside them, the kinds of cars they drive, the clothes they wear, the amount of money they have, or what is most convenient at the moment. She wonders whether we're losing our religion, substituting consumerism for faith because our identity has changed to that of being consumers.

Most of us receive more than three thousand messages every day via advertising in all its many forms. These messages create much of the discontent, insecurity, and fear within us. Every day we're told *who we're not*—we're not famous, we're not beautiful, we're not brilliant, we're not rich … *enough*, and therefore we're not worth as much as someone else. Because the identity and religion of consumerism are all about me, me, me, we are separated from our identity as the followers of Jesus, and that contributes to our dis-ease of spirit, a breakdown in community, and disinterest in the world around us.

Bill McKibben, an acclaimed environmental writer, once subjected himself to the experiment of watching 2,400 hours of videotape of everything that came across all the channels of the largest cable network during a twenty-four-hour period.[6] He must have been bombarded with newscasts and fluff pieces, game shows and talk shows, ads and infomercials, televangelists and Brady Bunch episodes. At the end of the week, there was "this one overriding message: You are the most important thing on earth. You, sitting there on the couch, clutching the remote, are the center of creation, the heaviest object in the known universe; all things orbit your desires. This Bud's for You."[7]

When we are the center of the universe, we feel that we deserve everything, and our identity as consumers makes us feel grossly inadequate, unfocused, agitated, and alone. But in nature, the opposite effect occurs as we consider the handiwork of God, learn more about the world around us, and are reminded that we are not the center of the universe. In God's creation we become more peaceful, more clear-headed, and the universe gets bigger than just our own small world, yet in a way that doesn't diminish us but rather helps us feel connected, often more connected to God and others.

Jesus tells us who we are. When we consider the birds and the lilies of the field, when we are connected to the natural world around us, we are reminded of who we really are. Jesus says that God cares for the birds and the lilies of the field, but more than that, God cares for us. We are God's beloved. When we remember who we are, we become more Christlike, more holy, and more just. Therefore we're better able to act out of our beloved selves and love God and our neighbor. Jesus' teaching isn't about making a commitment to abject poverty, but about having a change in attitude and having priorities about how we live so that no one on earth is without and all have enough. When we recognize that our identity is not as consumers, but as beloved children of God, we can strive and worry less.

The world's messages tell us what *we don't have*: we don't have the latest technology, fashion, entertainment, media, opportunity, money—or *enough* of it all. We discover ourselves in the same predicament as Adam and Eve that we find in the third chapter of Genesis. Let's review the story. God gave Adam and Eve the run of the Garden of Eden. Pretty nice deal; they didn't have to work or worry about what they would eat or wear. God made it clear with one rule: not to consume everything in sight, specifically fruit from the tree in the middle of the garden.

That shouldn't have been too hard to do! They had everything they could possibly need in order to live, and all they had to do was limit their desire and consumption. Yet we all know that they ate the fruit they were instructed not to eat. The original sin of Adam and Eve was to consume what wasn't theirs to consume. Did you ever think of the original sin as being an act of consuming what isn't ours to consume?

The consequences of disobeying God and consuming what wasn't theirs resulted in their being thrown out of the garden and experiencing disaster:

> Cursed is the ground because of you;
>> in toil you shall eat of it all the days of your life;

> thorns and thistles it shall bring forth for you;
> and you shall eat the plants of the field.
> By the sweat of your face you shall eat bread
> until you return to the ground. (Genesis 3:17b-19a)

Disobedience to God is connected to "thorns and thistles," a lack of fruitfulness of the land or desert. Throughout the history of the people of Israel, their failure to keep the commandments of God resulted in the devastation of the earth. The Scriptures repeatedly describe faithfulness as fruitfulness of the land and unfaithfulness as devastation of the land. This is one representative passage:

> I looked on the earth, and lo, it was waste and void;
> and to the heavens, and they had no light.
> I looked on the mountains, and lo, they were quaking,
> and all the hills moved to and fro.
> I looked, and lo, there was no one at all,
> and all the birds of the air had fled.
> I looked, and lo, the fruitful land was a desert,
> and all its cities were laid in ruins
> before the Lord, before his fierce anger.
> For thus says the Lord: The whole land shall be a
> desolation. (Jeremiah 4:23-27a)

Just as God "saw" that it was good in the creation story, now God "looks" and it is "waste," "void," "ruins," and "desolation." This passage nearly parallels the ordering of creation, but it's a *reversal* of the fruitfulness of creation—and the Lord is angry!

Conversely, hope is in obedience and faithfulness to God, and the result is the blessings of the fruitfulness of the earth. God declared,

> I will give you your rains in their season, and the land
> shall yield its produce, and the trees of the field shall
> yield their fruit. Your threshing shall overtake the vin-
> tage, and the vintage shall overtake the sowing; you
> shall eat your bread to the full, and live securely in your
> land. (Leviticus 26:4-5)

Disobedience and judgment came when people worshiped fertility gods. For years when I read the Prophets, I wondered why people would abandon God to worship fertility gods. Then I began to understand that these fertility gods promised prosperity and success. The people didn't necessarily stop believing in God; they worshiped other gods for added protection for prosperity and success.

As Christians today, we are tempted to foster this same sense of worshiping other gods of success, affluence, and materialism, and sometimes what is called the prosperity gospel is preached.[8] Over the last generation, an approach to the gospel promises wealth to Christians who take big risks for what their hearts desire and who trust God to work it out because they believe God wants them to have new homes or material possessions. This kind of consumerism has destroyed lives, and some say it contributed to the economic downturn of 2008. Jesus actually cautions us to limit both our desire and our consumption. Think about what the word *consumption* once meant. It referred to a disease causing the body to waste away. Our earth-body is wasting away as it suffers from our overconsumption, literally from our false identity as consumers, as we worship prosperity at the expense of others and earth's resources!

Jesus instructed his followers not to strive for these things. To *strive* is to be in a struggle with another. Striving puts us at odds with those who don't have enough, who suffer from the consequences of our unrestrained and unlimited consumption. When former vice president Al Gore won the Nobel Peace Prize in 2007, many people didn't understand how someone who was advocating for the health of the earth could receive a peace prize. What was the connection between peace and the planet? Peace and the planet are intimately connected when we are striving for more and depriving others of what they need. The results are violence, warfare, and further disaster.

Jesus reminded his first-century and now his twenty-first-century followers about *what we do have*. Life is about more than food and clothing, the material things of life. It's about the abundance and the goodness of life that God alone gives us: our lives, our health, our families and relationships of all kinds, this earth, our church, and our communities. When we remember what we do have, we limit our use of what God has given to us so that all may enjoy the goodness of God's creation. Instead of striving to consume resources, we are meant to strive for a deeper meaning of life with God, other human beings, and even creation itself. When we do that, locally and globally, we will have a sustainable existence as a people on earth and a greater potential for peace.

The messages of the world also tell us w*hat we can't do*. The world tells us that we can't make a difference or solve the problems of our communities, states, nation, and world. The mantra of what we can't do lies within us, and so we give up, despair, and grow cynical and cranky (to say the least). This is a major concern in the care for the earth because it's so difficult for us to change our lifestyles. It's uncertain whether we have enough time to make significant changes in order to provide hope for the future.

But Jesus reminds his listeners about *what they can do*. First, he tells them not to worry. Usually when people worry, they aren't very productive. Worrying is not acting; it keeps us from acting. Worry comes from despair and is not empowering. It literally means to strangle, twist, and choke. What's being strangled? When we worry, our priorities and values are twisted, and life-giving power that can make a positive difference is choked off.

The God who creates the birds of the air and the lilies of the field is the same God who is able to empower us to do what seems impossible: to feed the hungry, heal the sick, and live each day with hope and joy even as we face adversities and challenges. Jesus' life and message bring the hope and way to empower us to be better stewards of the earth.

Jesus' teaching calls us to stop regarding our identity as consumers, consumed by wanting more, and then striving, worrying, or stressing to fulfill our identity as consumers and being rendered incapable of solving the problems of our times, such as our dependence on fossil fuels. Together we can make a difference in these seemingly insurmountable problems in our world today.

An Inspiring Example

One of Sarah's friends decided she wanted to go to India and eventually to a monastery in North Dakota to work on her spiritual growth, seeking enlightenment and wisdom. She wanted to become more open and enlightened to the bigger picture of life, grounded in who she is and what her place is in life.

In preparing to go, she decided that she had too much stuff, and having so much stuff was in conflict with her values, who she wanted to be and what she wanted to do. So she started to give it all away. In general, it felt good to purge herself of her stuff. But she had the most difficulty in giving away her jeans.

Somehow her jeans were connected to her identity. What was her place or her niche in life? How did she fit into the larger picture? Was she wearing what everyone else was wearing to fit in? Was she doing what everyone else was doing in order to fit in? Or was she really living out who she is, finding her own niche in life?

She went on her spiritual quest, and when she returned, she found her niche (at least for now), helping other people purge themselves of their stuff so that they can better live out their identity, less determined by what others have and more determined by who they are.

Continuing the Journey—Do Good

In chapter 1, we learned the first of John Wesley's "three simple rules" for living. But to do no harm is only the first step. The second is to do good. I like Eugene Peterson's translation of the prophet Isaiah: "Learn to do good" (Isaiah 1:17 *THE MESSAGE*). We hope that reading this book will be a part of learning to do good. Wesley described "doing good" as "being in every kind merciful after their power; as they have opportunity, doing good of every possible sort, and, as far as possible, to all."[9] Learning to do good is being mindful of how our lifestyle, habits, and practices affect the lives of others and being merciful as we "have opportunity."

Doing good might involve learning what you can do without, as Sarah's Laura did. Or it might be recognizing your identity as Jesus reminds you *who you are, what you do have,* and *what you can do.*

Remember at the beginning of the chapter the story about the man who had the beautiful home? Don't you think that if the son had worked at cleaning it up, caring for it, and showing it to his father again in a much improved way that the father would know the son loved him—loved him enough to do something about the mess, offering the house back to the father as a sign of that love?

"Consider the lilies, how they grow: they neither toil nor spin; yet I tell you, even Solomon in all his glory was not clothed like one of these" (Luke 12:27). Jesus considered the earth, and, therefore, so should we.

A Commitment

What are some ways that you can be more proactive in caring for the earth? What good can you do? What good can you learn and then do? Find small ways to personally make a difference.

CHAPTER 3
The Love of Stuff

A man is rich in the proportion to the number of things which he can afford to let alone.

— **Henry David Thoreau**

Too Much for One Canoe

A young Chippewayan woman ventured to the city but eventually felt that she needed to return to her northern Canadian Indian reserve. She missed a simpler life, rooted in the seasons of the earth and being with her family. As she was preparing to leave her job in the city, she began to pack up her belongings, taking pictures off the walls and beddings off the bed and rugs off the floor, boxing up her books and clothes and beautiful, newly acquired dishes, and other household furnishings.

As she packed things up, she was thinking what her old friends would think of all her new and fancy acquisitions, enjoying the thought of how impressed they would be with the cache she had acquired over the few years she had been gone.

Exhausted, with the last box packed, she fell asleep and dreamed. In her dream, she was standing by the great Red River with all her packed boxes around her as she waited for her brother to pick her up in a canoe to take her home. She waited and waited until finally she saw him coming along the river in a small canoe.

She was happy to see him, and they greeted each other with warm affection and enthusiasm. But then her brother looked at all the boxes surrounding her, surprised at his sister's accumulation of goods. He began to carry box after box and put them into the canoe, filling the canoe in no time. Soon the canoe was filled to overflowing, and there were still more boxes on the shore.

She was upset at why her brother didn't bring a bigger canoe! But her brother reminded her that their grandmother said she was sure that one small canoe would be enough. At mention of their grandmother, she remembered the last conversation that they had had before she left home.

> Her grandmother had said then, "Remember my dear one, that if, when you come home from your adventure in the big city, you have more things to move than can fill one canoe, then you will know that you have become greedy. You will have taken more than your share and others will not have enough. If you need more than one canoe for your belongings, then you'll know that you have left behind the sacred traditions of your elders and have accepted the white man's ways. Don't let that happen to you, my granddaughter.[1]

At the memory of the conversation, she was filled with remorse. She realized that she had changed more than she would admit. Tears came to her eyes and she was filled with dismay.

But then she knew what she needed to do. She would give away all her extra belongings so that she could return in the one small canoe her brother had brought to pick her up. Having stuff is self-centered, Sarah says. Who says she doesn't know her Bible?

Jesus talked about money and wealth more than about heaven and eternal life. Or maybe it would be better to say that for Jesus there was some connection between money/wealth and heaven/eternal life:

> Someone in the crowd said to him, "Teacher, tell my brother to divide the family inheritance with me." But he said to him, "Friend, who set me to be a judge or ar-

bitrator over you?" And he said to them, "Take care! Be on your guard against all kinds of greed; for one's life does not consist in the abundance of possessions." Then he told them a parable: "The land of a rich man produced abundantly. And he thought to himself, 'What should I do, for I have no place to store my crops?' Then he said, 'I will do this: I will pull down my barns and build larger ones, and there I will store all my grain and my goods. And I will say to my soul, Soul, you have ample goods laid up for many years; relax, eat, drink, be merry.' But God said to him, 'You fool! This very night your life is being demanded of you. And the things you have prepared, whose will they be?' So it is with those who store up treasures for themselves but are not rich toward God." (Luke 12:13-21)

The man's presenting concern to Jesus was that he was being unfairly denied what should come to him as an inheritance and Jesus should put a stop to this injustice. Jesus wanted to know why the man made him his judge. A rabbi played the role of judge, but did he really want Jesus to be his judge in the matter? Maybe, as we say, the man didn't really want to go there.

Take care! Be on your guard against all kinds of greed; for one's life does not consist in the abundance of possessions. (Luke 12:15)

Instead of arbitrating the family dispute, Jesus went to the heart of the matter: greed. As Eugene Peterson says, Jesus "ignores the man's 'rights' and skewers the man's greed."[2] *Greed* is a word that makes us very uncomfortable. Most of us, when hearing the word, conclude that it doesn't apply to us. So let's just call greed "the love of stuff."

To open the man's heart, Jesus told a story that invited him to face his love of stuff. It's a story about a farmer whose dream comes true: a bumper crop. What should he do with his unexpected good fortune? He decides the obvious thing: he will tear down the puny barns he has and build bigger barns. He'll store his crop and live high on the hog for a long time.

As we analyze the story, we see exactly what Sarah means when she says that stuff makes us selfish. The farmer says in short order: "I will...I will...I will...." He gets some wealth and suddenly it's all about his will: what will he do with his stuff? He loses all mindfulness of others.

Little wonder that God says to him, "Fool!" When I was growing up, *fool* was a word we weren't supposed to call anyone. It was like calling someone stupid today; it's not nice, and it's a word that can hurt or cause someone to believe less about himself or herself (not to mention you!). But in the Bible, calling someone a fool has a bit more bite to it. In Psalm 14:1 we read:

> Fools say in their hearts, "There is no God."
> They are corrupt, they do abominable deeds;
> there is no one who does good.

So biblical fools are people who don't believe in God, and as a result their lives are corrupt and they "do abominable deeds." At this point the man must feel like his head is spinning! How did he go from being the victim in his own story to being a fool doing abominable things in Jesus' story? Soon his head will be exploding!

For most of us, building bigger barns hardly seems to be an abominable act. I doubt too many sermons have been preached on literally building bigger barns. What about bigger houses? What about bigger churches? Even bigger sanctuaries? Bigger, better, more luxurious anything? *Bigger, better, more*: these have been the watchwords of our culture. If we're progressing in bigger, better, and more, then we must be doing well in life! Yet Jesus seems to have a different view.

The story is meant to step on all our toes, not just those of this hapless man who wanted Jesus to simply say that the man was being treated unfairly so he could go home and be reasonably upset at his brother for this injustice. Isn't that what we want from Jesus, too? We want Jesus to salve our sense of injustice about how we don't have as much or bigger or better or more than someone else.

Are we looking at ourselves yet?

The economic downturn of 2008 caused many Americans to come face-to-face with the overconsumption of goods in their lives, especially as it affected credit card spending and debt—the "something for nothing" mind-set, getting a good deal today that they didn't think through well enough to know how to pay for it tomorrow.

During the beginning of the Great Recession, all I could think of was that silly saying of Wimpy from the Popeye cartoons of my childhood: "I'll gladly pay you on Tuesday for a hamburger today." I don't know, but I wonder if it was funny forty or fifty years ago, because nobody would give anybody a hamburger today if no payment was to be made until next Tuesday. In the midst of the declining economy, it was apparent that we had built a society on the expectation that we could have all the hamburgers we wanted and we didn't have to pay for them until next Tuesday or the Tuesday after that or the Tuesday after that or whenever, maybe never.

Eugene Peterson describes greed, or our love of stuff, as a virus that overtakes us like an infection.[3] It's as if the virus greed worms its way into the imagination, causing us to imagine that we need things. It crawls into our eyes, seeing every new thing that comes flying onto the TV or computer screen to entice us to want, want, want in order to buy, buy, buy. It gives us a heart attack when we think we just can't live without something that we have our hearts set on.

Author Adam Hamilton points out in his book *Enough* that

> three of the seven deadly sins relate directly to the problem we have with money and possessions. First, we are afflicted by envy or covetousness. We want what others have, and we will do whatever we can to get it—whether that means taking it or buying it for ourselves. Second, we are afflicted by greed or avarice. We have an intense desire for more and don't want to share what we have. And third, we are afflicted with gluttony. We keep consuming, even when we are full and our needs are met—and we finally make ourselves sick.[4]

And deeper and deeper in debt. Peterson and Hamilton use the analogy of disease, and the dis-ease is in our relationships with God and others. Therefore the man's actions in Jesus' story will be corrupt and abominable because "I will...I will...I will" denies others entrance into his heart. Jesus makes it clear in his parable that when we strive for money and possessions we minimize the importance of the relationships in our lives. The perceived injustice between the man and his brother has ruptured the man's relationship with one meant to be closest to him.

We ascribe an emotional value to a lot of our stuff. That's often what makes it so difficult to throw out, re-gift, or simply know what to do with it. Our memories are locked in the stuff instead of in our hearts and minds.

Then there is the emotionality of giving gifts. Too often gift giving is a way of saying, "I love you," but the gift isn't desired or appreciated. It becomes extra stuff. What do you do with all the tchotchkes? We waste money (better to give to a worthy cause) and fill our lives with stuff because someone gave it to us. As Christians, how can we better give to those we love?

Acquiring stuff keeps us separated from our literal neighbors as well as neighbors around the world. Jesus didn't use the word *neighbor* in this story, but he made it clear that ultimately our greed, or love of stuff, "divides the family." The separation into the haves and have-nots comes from a fundamental love of stuff. We ponder what would break down the barriers between the haves and have-nots as if it were an economic question instead of a question of "who is my neighbor?"

Could it be that connecting Jesus and the environment is so controversial because it challenges an American core value: individualism? Individualism is in opposition to the ways in which Jesus wants us to live. Throughout the following chapters on waste, water, and food in this book, you'll discover that when we practice more environmentally sound behaviors and make changes to our lifestyle, we rediscover more and more community in our lives.

Bill McKibben has given voice to the reality that we are more isolated from our neighbors. He's puzzled about why Christianity hasn't been more on the forefront of addressing what we're doing to our earthly home, too. He says:

> It's almost mandatory... that the churches help lead the way. Mandatory because by now this is a theological issue... because taking on climate change would mean taking on the central unchristian element of American culture: its wild individualism. More than anything else, fossil fuel has allowed us to stop being neighbors to each other, both literally—we move ever farther into ever emptier suburbs—and figuratively—we depend

less and less on each other for anything real. . . . The crisis we face is at least as morally urgent as the civil rights movement.[5]

McKibben challenges Christians to address the "selfish individualism that has come to define too much of our culture."[6] "Wild individualism" makes us care more about our stuff than about our neighbors, near and far, now and in the future, and therefore alienates us not only from our neighbor, but also from God.

Jesus has a lot to say about our accumulation of and reliance on material wealth because it affects how we relate to God. If we place our trust and security in God, we have less need for things that do not last. By calling the man in the parable a fool, Jesus was also implying that the man missed out on his relationship with God, no longer trusting God but trusting in bigger barns. Greed, or love of stuff, reveals that we are placing our trust in material and earthly things, but more accurately it means that we're living as if there is no God; that fool idea raises its head again. We might say we believe in God, but we're acting out of a

> **Greed, or love of stuff, reveals that we are placing our trust in material and earthly things, but more accurately it means that we're living as if there is no God.**

functional atheism, trusting in what we can see instead of investing in what will last—even eternally.

And by eternally, I do mean life with God forever, but I also mean that which lasts beyond our lives on earth.

"OK, OK, I get the greed thing," you may be saying, "but what does greed have to do with ecology?"

Consider the Science of Stuff

Greed or love of stuff causes us to accumulate more than we need at the expense of others, our neighbors near and far. We don't always connect our overconsumption with others' lack of basics and, even as you'll see in the next chapter, the way they are relegated to live in our waste.

To begin with, we have a lot of people on earth. The population of the earth is estimated to reach 7 billion by June 2012. Currently 5.4 billion or more people live in developing countries such as Nigeria, Ethiopia, India, China, Mexico, and Bangladesh, and these developing countries account for 97 percent of the world's population growth. India alone adds around 18.6 million people per year. Approximately 1.2 billion live in developed countries such as the United States, Japan, and Germany. In contrast to India, the United States is projected to add about 3 million people to its population in a given year. This breakdown gives the impression that the overpopulation of this planet is an issue of the developing world. It would seem that to curb the world population, changes must occur with the developing nations. They are the problem, right? If only they could be more like us, more developed.

With less than 20 percent of the world's total population, developed countries such as the United States use 88 percent of the world's natural resources and create 75 percent of the world's waste. If India and China developed into nations that consume at U.S. levels, we would need two additional planets of earth to deal with their resource and waste needs. Currently one person in the United States consumes as much as thirty people in India. Instead of comparing the 18.6 million additional Indians each year to the 3 million additional Americans, we would be more accurate in terms of consumption to think of it as 18.6 million versus 90 million (if we consume thirty times as much, then it would be 3 million times 30 equals 90 million). Is the developing world the problem, or is the finger more aptly pointed at us? And what do we do when poor countries dream to be more like us? Is the developed world setting an example that is even remotely sustainable?

It comes down to consumption. The developed world consumes resources and produces waste at an alarming rate. Look around you. Stuff is everywhere. This book is stuff. You're probably sitting on some stuff. You're in a house or an office or a coffee shop; all of it is filled with stuff! Stuff gets you from one place to another; there's the stuff of a car or a bike or even a pair of shoes.

The stuff a civilization leaves behind when it's gone tells us what it was like, how people lived, what they valued. We put the stuff of ancient people on display. We study their stuff. But how much do we know about our stuff? How often do we look around at our stuff and ask: What are we like? How do we live? What do we value?

Our stuff tells our story. If we seek to truly understand ourselves, we must truly understand our stuff. What is stuff made of? Who makes our stuff, and where is it made? How do we get stuff? How do we choose what stuff we need? Where does our stuff go when we no longer want or need it? Does it just go away?

In the brilliant and informative short, free, downloadable film *The Story of Stuff*,[7] Annie Leonard explains the process of stuff: the steps of extraction, production, distribution, consumption, and disposal. Examination of these steps gives us the information to understand our stuff and ourselves.

Extraction

Stuff comes from somewhere. Making our stuff ultimately requires resources that are already present—*natural* resources.[8] The United States makes up roughly 5 percent of the world's population but uses 30 percent of the world's resources.[9] These resources are not all located within the United States. They often come from developing countries. Extracting these resources often places human lives at risk, especially if there aren't strict labor laws to protect people.

Because fossil fuels (such as coal, oil, and natural gas) and minerals (such as copper, iron, sand, and the components of steel) are buried in the earth's crust, extracting them involves intensive damage to the ecosystem above what is being mined. In addition, once the resource is extracted, it is difficult, if not impossible, to return the earth to its original condition.

Developing countries often have the natural resources that developed countries desire, and selling them to us at a profit would potentially help lift them out of poverty and allow them to develop their infrastructures, such as education and health care. Yet this rarely happens. Instead, we essentially steal the natural resources from the people living right on top of them. Even when the first world pays, the amount is not what the resources are actually worth. The payment may be in exchange for minimal debts, it may be a meager amount to a few local people, or it may be a larger amount to just a few top officials who relocate poor persons living in the area to be mined. The point is this: the extreme demands of the industrially developed world do not benefit the people of the third world, even when the third world possesses the precious, limited, and rare natural resources required by the wealthy. The extraction process, the first step in creating stuff, hurts poor people, hurts the third world, and hurts the planet.

Production

The production of stuff is the process where natural resources are combined with energy and with chemicals to produce goods. More than 100,000 different synthetic chemicals are in or are used to make our stuff. There has been minimal testing of the health impacts of these chemicals and no testing of their synergistic effects. Toxic, brominated, flame-retardant chemicals are put in and on our couches, computers, appliances, carpet, and a host of other products. Four billion tons of toxic chemicals are released into the environment every year (and that is only what is reported). These chemicals end up in our air, our water, and eventually our bodies through what we breathe, drink, and eat. Factory workers are at greatest risk. One would assume that a person who does this work must be paid an incredibly high wage. How else would one convince a person to work in such an environment? Just as the poor in the third world aren't paid for their precious resources, the poor are exploited as workers in stuff-making factories.[10]

The poor do some of the hardest, most dangerous work for the longest hours and minimal pay because they do not have a choice. The rich of the first world purposefully employ, either in America or overseas, the most desperate of our world to do some of the most dangerous work. Production of stuff hurts poor people, takes advantage of the third world, and pollutes the planet.

Distribution

The resources to make stuff and the stuff itself travel all around the globe. In *The Story of Stuff* Annie Leonard talked about a $4.99 radio she saw for sale in a store. She wondered where one could make a radio that cost only $4.99. It is entirely possible that the metal of the radio was mined in South Africa, the oil was drilled out of Iraq, and the plastic and assembly occurred in China; then the product was sold in the United States. The travel of the pieces alone should cost more than the $4.99 price, not to mention the people along the way who would be paid for each of the component parts, for the assembly, for the transportation, for the shelf space, and for the sale of the radio, right? The key is that someone did pay for what we regard as a cheap radio. The people in the countries where the mining took place paid, the people who built the radio paid, and the minimum-wage employee at the big-box mart where the radio was sold so cheaply paid. All of those people pitched in so that the radio could cost $4.99.

Consumption

The key to the process of making stuff is selling stuff. The fourth step, consumption, has changed markedly since the end of World War II when economic voices stated that the primary purpose of the American economy was to produce more consumer goods. Economist Victor Labow laid it out perfectly when he said,

> Our enormously productive economy demands that we make consumption our way of life, that we convert the buying and use of goods into rituals, that we seek our spiritual satisfaction in consumption.... We need things consumed, burned up, replaced, and discarded at an ever accelerating rate.[11]

This goal was achieved through perceived and planned obsolescence. Planned obsolescence is the creation of stuff that is designed to be used only once and then replaced. Mop-head refills, bottled water containers, disposable coffee cups, and plastic sandwich bags are all blatant examples, but even computers and other electronics fit into planned obsolescence. Think of how infrequently we update or repair our existing electronics. If a TV breaks or if a computer fries, we shop for a new one. Doing this often makes economic sense because paying for repairs can be almost as costly as buying a new and updated version of the broken electronic device, which is not accidental. Perceived obsolescence is the idea that what you have needs to be replaced even if it still works. Planned and perceived obsolescence is part of all of the stuff in our society today. Stuff is not made to last or to be worn out. Consider how infrequently we wear out our clothes, as opposed to getting new clothes that are more in style. Styles change to create the perception that what we already have no longer "works."

Added to this new system of consumption is the pressure to have *more* things. In our society, we show our success through our stuff. The cars we drive, the size of our houses, the stuff in our houses, and the clothes we wear are reflections of how much we have and therefore how successful we are to the world around us. This is not coincidental either. Only 1 percent of distributed goods are in use six months later.[12] That statistic is astonishing. Almost nothing in the grand scheme of what we buy is used six months after we get it.

Disposal

The fact that so little of what we consume remains after months later explains how on average each American produces 4.5 pounds of garbage or waste per day. This waste fills landfills, thus polluting the land. Landfills produce copious amounts of methane, which pollutes the air and exerts a more powerful greenhouse effect than carbon dioxide. Incinerated waste releases toxic chemicals such as dioxins (the most toxic man-made substance). In fact, incinerators are the number one source of dioxins released into the air.

Recycling is great, but it is hardly the answer. So much of what we consume is not recyclable, and much of what is intended for recycling is not recycled. For instance, less than 10 percent of plastic water bottles are recycled, and Americans consume half a billion bottles of water per week. Also, recycling requires resources such as energy and water, and it does not address the waste, pollution, use of resources, and effects on other life (including workers).

The structure of our consumptive society harms the poor people of this world; destroys ecosystems; pollutes air, water, and land; and uses valuable resources. If all countries consumed and disposed at the rate that Americans do, we would need three to five more earths to sustain life.[13] The mentality of consumption is fairly new in our society. In our system of constant consumption and our disposable society, driven by the perceived and even planned need for more and a focus on the best deals, who is paying and who is profiting? Where would Jesus shop? What would Jesus buy?

Consider T-shirts. Everyone has a T-shirt or two or twenty, right? Twenty-five million tons of cotton are used to make T-shirts every year. Just over eight million tons of insecticides are used to produce those twenty-five million tons of cotton. That's one-third of a pound of insecticides for every one pound of cotton! It then takes loads of fossil fuel energy to bale, fluff, and press the cotton into a form that can be used as fabric. Once the material is ready, chlorine is used to bleach it, even if it's going to be dyed another color later. Formaldehyde (yes, the same stuff used on frogs in biology class) is used to make the fabric soft and wrinkle resistant. The process up to this point requires approximately 256 gallons of water per T-shirt! Most T-shirts are made in sweatshops in China, Mexico, the Philippines, Haiti, or Taiwan. Sweatshop workers, typically young women, are paid between 10¢ and 13¢ per hour and work ten or more hours per day. Haitian workers have battled for $3.75 a day, the highest pay of sweatshop workers.

The structure of our consumptive society harms the poor people of this world; destroys ecosystems; pollutes air, water, and land; and uses valuable resources. If all countries consumed and disposed at the rate that Americans do, we would need three to five more earths to sustain life.

How often when we buy a T-shirt for $5.00 or $10.00 do we consider the insecticides used to grow the cotton, the energy and water resources used to turn it into fabric, the chemical pollution of bleach and formaldehyde and dyes that make it the T-shirt fabric we desire, and the people who work ten hours for $1.30 to $3.75 per day to sew the shirt?

After T-shirts are made, they go on an ocean cruise of thousands of miles and then another journey of thousands of miles by trucks and trains to the destinations where they will be sold. These forms of transportation use fossil fuels, so there is a carbon price tag on the T-shirt beyond the amount that we may pay. How many of these T-shirts do we need? How many do we buy? Why do we buy them?

Consider the waste. We keep only 21 percent of our annual clothing purchases for a year. Americans throw away more than sixty-eight pounds per person of clothing and textiles per year, suggesting that we know we don't need or want all this stuff. The world's supply of women's clothing is seven times that of men's.

How often do you consider the resources, pollution, and people involved in what we buy, whether it's T-shirts, bottled water, cell phones, or food? What's the real cost of these items? And who has already paid for those costs or will pay in the future? The earth pays, poor people pay, and future generations pay.

Jesus' teaching questions why we want more, bigger, and better. Of course we require some stuff in order to live, but we need to limit our stuff. More, bigger, and better aren't healthy for our hearts as those desires crowd out our love for our neighbors and the environment.

An Inspiring Example

When we make a major change or experience a transition in life—for example, we relocate, we buy a new home, or we retire—we have an opportunity to prioritize our lives so as to live in a more ecologically friendly and neighborly way.

When United Methodist bishop Sharon Brown Christopher retired, she and her husband researched carefully where they wanted to live. They had never chosen the house they lived in throughout their married life because both were clergy and they always had lived in a parsonage.

They considered the usual priorities of retirement in terms of their selection of a place, a house, and a community: near family, friends, educational opportunities, and medical facilities; a culturally diverse area; and a desirable climate. But they also wanted to reduce their carbon footprint by rightsizing their space to their lifestyle. They wanted space that they would actually need and use, so they purchased a condo.

They chose a neighborhood where they could walk to many of their destinations, such as the grocery store, pharmacy, bank, doctors, dentist, exercise arenas, restaurants, a big-box store that had most of the things they needed, and a favorite coffee shop. They could be anywhere in the city by car within ten or fifteen minutes, and public transportation was a block away from their home.

Continuing the Journey—Stay in Love with God

John Wesley's final "rule" for living a faithful life that is transformative, life-giving, and sustaining is to stay in love with God through means of keeping up spiritual practices, or "ordinances."

Although staying in love with God may feel like a stretch for some in light of caring for the earth, nothing could be farther from the truth. Caring for the earth can be considered a way of staying in love with God because it includes practices that "bind us to God every day but [it] also include[s] actions that heal the pain, injustice, and inequality of our world. It is impossible to stay in love with God and not desire to see God's goodness and grace shared with the entire world."[14] And I suggest that "the entire world" includes the earth itself as well as the peoples who live on it now and in the future.

Staying in love with God means practicing the means that keep us connected to God, such as Scripture reading, prayer, fasting, Communion, and worship. Staying in love with God also means to live and practice care for the earth that God gave us and entrusted to us. Would spending more time outside, taking a walk, and making the effort to watch the cycles of the moon and the turning of the seasons actually help you face the stress and strain of life? Could doing these things give you more time to reflect on God and your life, praying and listening for the ways that God would have you change some habits in your life?

Perhaps in this chapter you identified somewhat with the man who built bigger barns to store his excess of wealth. Perhaps you suffer from the love of stuff, too. Don't we all? We must remember that inextricably linked with staying in love with God is loving our neighbors, near and far, rich and poor.

A Commitment

Focus on loving God and others more than your possessions. Work on your attentiveness to appreciating what you *have* rather than what you *lack*. In what ways can the reflection on and examination of your life, the changes you can make, and the good you can learn help you stay in love with God?

CHAPTER 4
Creating Hell All around Us

When you live in a cocktail of heavy metals or chemicals,
your body struggles every day to survive.
— Richard Fuller, head of Blacksmith Institute, an
environmental nonprofit

In the award-winning movie *Slumdog Millionaire*, Jamal Malik is an eighteen-year-old orphan from the slums of Mumbai. He has found his way onto the game show *Who Wants to Be a Millionaire?* but he's so smart he arouses the suspicion that he is cheating, so the authorities arrest him. In the course of explaining to the police why he wanted to be on the show—which didn't have to do with the money—he tells his life story and the viewer is introduced to him as a street kid who has grown up in a slum, specifically a garbage dump in Mumbai. Horribly graphic scenes depict Jamal and his brother living in the dump before they encounter the many adventures that eventually lead Jamal to the girl he loves.

Viewers in America found the film to be truly inspiring because a young man emerges from the dump, yet we forget that children live and grow up in all kinds of garbage dumps around the world with little possibility of going on a game show to find their way out. But at least *Slumdog Millionaire* introduced us to the reality of the living hell that real children and their families encounter.

Throughout the world, in

The poorest of the poor live in the stuff discarded by wealthy people. This is a reality all over the world.

Cambodia, Thailand, Iraq, Guatemala, Brazil, and other places, hundreds and thousands of children live in garbage dumps. *New York Times* editorialist Nicholas D. Kristof describes life for children in a

Phnom Penh, Cambodia, dump:

> This is a Dante-like vision of hell. It's a mountain of festering refuse, a half-hour hike across, emitting clouds of smoke from subterranean fires. The miasma of toxic stink leaves you gasping, breezes batter you with filth, and even the rats look forlorn. Then the smoke parts and you come across a child ambling barefoot, searching for old plastic cups that recyclers will buy for five cents a pound. Many families actually live in shacks on this smoking garbage.[1]

The poorest of the poor live in the stuff discarded by wealthy people. They create houses from scraps of metal and furnish them with household goods discarded to the dump. They spend their days wandering around the garbage, collecting recyclables for pennies apiece. Once they can walk, the children are also expected to scavenge. Sometimes children are run over by garbage trucks or crushed by trash dumping from trucks. This is a reality all over the world.

Why take us on a journey through this literal, modern-day hell? To help us understand the parable that Jesus told about hell and how it connects to what *our* consumption produces and its impact on the poorest of the poor, many of them children. Meet Lazarus:

> There was a rich man who was dressed in purple and fine linen and who feasted sumptuously every day. And at his gate lay a poor man named Lazarus, covered with sores, who longed to satisfy his hunger with what fell from the rich man's table; even the dogs would come

and lick his sores. The poor man died and was carried away by the angels to be with Abraham. The rich man also died and was buried. In Hades, where he was being tormented, he looked up and saw Abraham far away with Lazarus by his side. He called out, "Father Abraham, have mercy on me, and send Lazarus to dip the tip of his finger in water and cool my tongue; for I am in agony in these flames." But Abraham said, "Child, remember that during your lifetime you received your good things, and Lazarus in like manner evil things; but now he is comforted here, and you are in agony. Besides all this, between you and us a great chasm has been fixed, so that those who might want to pass from here to you cannot do so, and no one can cross from there to us." He said, "Then, father, I beg you to send him to my father's house—for I have five brothers—that he may warn them, so that they will not also come into this place of torment." Abraham replied, "They have Moses and the prophets; they should listen to them." He said, "No, father Abraham; but if someone goes to them from the dead, they will repent." He said to him, "If they do not listen to Moses and the prophets, neither will they be convinced even if someone rises from the dead." (Luke 16:19-31)

Usually someone in extreme poverty remains anonymous. There is no poverty quite like not being given a name, rendering a person invisible and unimportant since we remember names of people who are important to us. But the striking aspect of this story is that the poor person is named—Lazarus—and is the only one named in the story told by Jesus. Over centuries, it's as if we can't stand *not* to call the rich man by his name, so one has been given in many commentaries, and it is Dives, which means "rich" in Latin. Mr. Rich it is, then!

Every detail about Mr. Rich screams consumption and luxury. He was clothed in purple and fine linen like the robes of the high priests. He feasted on fine foods. Yet most of us are more like Dives than we are like Lazarus in spite of our complaints about losing money in the stock market during the Great Recession or not having the latest electronic gadget. We acquire many luxuries and call them necessities. We dress in clothing that is made at the expense of others (remember the journey of the T-shirts). We feast on fine food, such as strawberries in January.

Lazarus, in contrast to Mr. Rich, was hungry and emaciated with ulcerated skin that produced sores, attracting dogs that came to lick them. Lazarus might have been too weak of body or spirit to even shoo away what were considered unclean animals. Like a child living in a garbage dump, Lazarus didn't appear to the religious elite of his day to have any future, much less an *eternal* future.

The custom of the time was that people who ate fine meals used chunks of bread as napkins to wipe their hands. The bread would be thrown away from the table where beggars like Lazarus would be waiting for these scraps to stave off hunger. Lazarus literally lived off the waste products that Dives threw away.

Dives did nothing to alleviate Lazarus's suffering. Like us, who may see poverty every day near or far away, Dives encountered him daily but never knew his name, never talked to him, and never reached out to him with food, clothing, shelter, or money, much less a kind word or a semblance of a relationship. There was a chasm between them that Mr. Rich never attempted to cross in Lazarus's lifetime. But as the old adage says, watch who you step on as you are on your way up because you may encounter them on your way down.

And down, down, down went Dives in the unexpected change of plot. Both Dives and Lazarus died and went to their respective rewards. Contrary to what either one of them might have anticipated, or the listeners of this story would expect, Lazarus was sitting cool as a cucumber up in heaven, and Dives was in the sweatshop in hell. Dives's sin was that he didn't care about Lazarus, since Dives did nothing for a fellow human being in extreme need.

Hades, hell, and *Gehenna* were words used in early Jewish and Christian times to describe the place where people like Dives went after they died, if they had been wicked. The name *Gehenna* comes from the place where refuse and unclean animals were burned outside the Gate of the Valley of the Old City of Jerusalem. The smell of the dump would have been evident when the winds brought it toward the beautiful city of God.

In the Hebrew Scriptures, Gehenna was an actual place where other gods were worshiped, involving the *sacrifice of children.* Children were passed through fire as a part of the worship to the god Molech. When King Josiah discovered the Law after it had been lost for many years, he insisted that this practice was an abomination and that it be stopped because the Law forbade the worshiping of an idol and the sacrificing of children in the fires of hell. Children sacrificed in a dump, then and now.

Hell is described in this story as an unbearably hot place without water, but worse yet for Mr. Rich was that from his place of torment he could see the comfort of Lazarus in heaven. Dives might not have seen Lazarus's condition before he died, but now Lazarus's condition was ever present before him. Dives lived as if there was absolutely no connection or responsibility toward Lazarus, and the result was a chasm between them in death as it was in life.

Dives begged Father Abraham to have his "good old friend" Lazarus send him down some bottled water (OK, I'm pushing the interpretation here a bit, but you get the idea). Dives still didn't see Lazarus as anything but his support crew, even in Hades. Lazarus was a child of God in the inner circle of divine grace who no longer had to live responding to Dives's whims.

Dives's request was denied, and so he began to bargain. He wanted Lazarus sent to his five brothers so that they didn't make the same mistake that he made in ignoring the needs of the poor around them. Father Abraham didn't think that it was Lazarus's job to return to earth to help out Dives's family and so kept Lazarus close to his bosom instead. Father Abraham told Dives that the purpose of the Law and the Prophets was meant to teach his brothers how to care for those in need, including the stranger, widows, and orphans (see Leviticus 19:9-10; Deuteronomy 15:7-11), and the poor and needy.

Again having his request denied, Dives insisted that if his brothers heard from someone who had been raised from the dead, they would come to their senses. They would immediately repent and change their equally callous ways, and they would be saved from torment in hell. That was particularly rich, so to speak, from Jesus' point of view because Dives was probably a Sadducee who did not believe in the resurrection of the dead. For Dives to suggest that a major change in behavior could be expected from someone being raised from the dead was highly unlikely and obviously self-serving!

This is a story ultimately about Dives's brothers. And we are his brothers. The questions are, who is our neighbor, and how do we relate to our neighbor? Or are we separated from our neighbors to the extent that while they live in hellish conditions—often brought about by our overconsumption and waste—we have no regard for them?

Surely Jesus told this parable for us as well as for the first-century followers to help us see and care for those who live in the garbage dumps of hell that we create on this earth and to eliminate our over-production of waste through changes in our policies, our lifestyles, and our practices so that we don't condemn ourselves to a world of pollution and waste of any kind.

What Makes Hell?

Pollution is the by-product of human industry, agriculture, and daily lifestyle. This waste can be toxic liquid chemicals, piles of solid trash, molecules of poisonous gases, used medical supplies, pesticide runoff, and many other toxic forms. It is waste, no longer needed in the process that produced it and no longer valuable to those discarding it, and it is often dangerous to those who touch it or live near it or are exposed to it in some way.

There exists a veil of separation between us, the garbage we set at the curb, and the planet and people who live in, live off, and are ultimately affected by our waste. Our lifestyle of throwaway living creates hells on this planet and for many of its people. To lift the veil is to see the reality between us and the people affected, including our own children who will inherit the earth.

Waste doesn't occur in nature. In nature, the by-product of one reaction, the unused material from one source, or the remains of a once living thing are the requirements of something else. Everything in nature is recycled! In the absence of humans, no piles of toxicity or garbage would exist. Humans, however, create waste, and this waste most often becomes pollution in the otherwise pristine planet.

Pollution is a problem. Pollution is dirty and unhealthy, and it is changing the planet in disturbing and significant ways. Pollution can be roughly grouped into land, air, and water pollution. In each of these broad areas, the damage done is immense. Although there could be many additional chapters dedicated exclusively to water and air pollution, we have chosen to focus on trash and how we are literally trashing our land. We do not mean to downplay water and air pollution, and we will work to tie them in when possible, but we thought we'd give the stuff we throw away center stage.

Our trash does not go to a magical "away" when we put it on the curb. Our garbage—the stuff, the resources, we throw out—goes into the air when incinerated or becomes methane when it is broken down in landfills, goes into the water as polluting leachate, goes into the ground as mountains of landfill garbage, goes into the oceans as enormous circulating islands of plastic, and goes to developing countries as man-made mineral mines for children and the poor to pick through. There exists a veil of separation between us, the garbage we set at the curb, and the planet and people who live in, live off, and are ultimately affected by our waste. Our lifestyle of throwaway living creates hells on this planet and for many of its people. To lift the veil is to see the reality between us and the people affected, including our own children who will inherit the earth.

Land Pollution

The United States, with only 4.6 percent of the world's population, creates one-third of its solid waste. Of this, approximately 38 percent is paper, 11 percent is food, 12 percent is yard waste, and 11 percent is plastic.[2] Each American produces 4.5 pounds of garbage per day! The vast majority of this is sent to one of our more than ten thousand landfills. We consume and discard, use and toss out, as if what we are doing truly doesn't matter. This solid waste is what we load into our garbage bins every week, what we set out on the curb at night, and what we assume magically goes away.

If each American produces an average of 4.5 pounds of garbage per day, what makes up this 31.5 pounds of garbage per person per week? Much of it is what I call routine garbage. It's the same old stuff we throw out pretty much every day.

Consider disposable coffee cups, for example. It is common to walk into any coffee shop, order a coffee to go, drink it down, and toss out the paper cup without ever considering how our morning coffee affects resources and creates waste on this planet. The paper companies estimate that in 2010 we will use 23 billion paper coffee cups. That translates into 14 million tons of wood from 9.4 million trees. Making the cups requires 8,500 Olympic-sized swimming pools worth of water, and the waste created as we toss them out adds up to 363 million pounds of solid waste. A quick response may be that we could recycle them, but that is a shortsighted approach. These cups are not recyclable. Their plastic inner coating renders them both less permeable to coffee leaks and nonrecyclable. Even if they were recyclable, recycling requires materials, energy, and water. Limiting what we use and recycling what we use are helpful, but they don't address the heart of the issue of our consumption and toss-out (into a recycle can or garbage can) lifestyle and they fail to truly lift the veil between what we do and the hellish consequences of our actions.

Americans throw away 25 billion Styrofoam cups each year,[3] which is enough to circle the earth 436 times. Nonrecyclable and nonbiodegradable cups are still being used in churches! Can we imagine offering Jesus some coffee in a Styrofoam cup if he visited our church?

Cups—paper or Styrofoam—are examples of some of the routine garbage we create. We could have focused on plastic bags (in 2002, 4.5 trillion plastic bags were produced), plastic wrap (every year we use enough to shrink-wrap Texas), and plastic containers for everything from laundry soap to motor oil to bottled water (Americans use 25 billion plastic bottles per year). The list goes on and on.

Landfills

The majority of what we throw out goes into landfills, holes in the earth. The United States has more than ten thousand landfills, and this number is increasing because trash is a highly profitable business and the United States has an abundance of open, cheap land.

U.S. federal regulations require all landfills to be in areas that are free of fault lines and away from bodies of water. These newer, sanitary landfills are lined with clay and plastic and then a second impermeable liner to collect leachate. Leachate is water that comes from or comes into contact with a landfill. As trash is added to the landfill, it is periodically covered with clay and plastic foam to reduce the risk of fire and to reduce odor. In addition, pipes are sometimes installed to capture and even use methane released from landfills. The world's largest landfill in New York produces enough methane that, if captured, could power twelve thousand homes. Although some of the ten thousand landfills utilize this technology, most do not, and methane is released freely from the dump or is burned off.[4]

Despite regulations and precautions, landfills are chemical time bombs. Eighty-six percent of all U.S. landfills have contaminated groundwater, and 20 percent of all Superfund (toxic) sites are former landfills.[5] Even with new technology, all landfills will eventually leak. Most landfills have a life span of around forty or fifty years.

So why then do we continue to dump our waste into the earth? Landfills are a profitable business. The profit in garbage is the main reason we do less recycling than we could. In general, recycling *costs* money while garbage *makes* money. Hundreds of millions of dollars are made in the United States on garbage alone.[6] Private garbage companies buy cheap land, often in the Midwest. This inexpensive land allows them to charge competitive prices, especially when compared to the prices in areas where land is more expensive. This setup encourages other states, as far away as Florida, to ship their garbage to landfills in Indiana and Michigan.[7] The scenario is similar in the state of Virginia, which has seven megafills to receive garbage from New York and other surrounding states where land is too expensive to make a landfill a viable waste solution.

The profit in garbage is the main reason we do less recycling than we could. In general, recycling *costs* money while garbage *makes* money.

Private companies buy land and then offer great deals for out-of-state and even international (Canadian) garbage. These private companies make profits from receiving and disposing of garbage at the expense of long-term environmental impact. There is not an incentive for them to do anything except fill the land with garbage, even toxic medical waste from a thousand miles away, and fill their pocketbooks instead of making the community a safer and better place to live or creatively thinking of ways to compost or recycle more.

The United States could compost 50 percent of what it currently dumps into landfills as garbage. Of the ten thousand landfills in the United States, roughly three hundred are set up for methane capture. If methane capture was installed at every dump, the United States would exceed the goals set forth by the Kyoto Protocol for greenhouse gas reduction. Composting and methane capture are practices that mimic nature. What is waste at the source is recycled and reused as a valuable input at another source.[8]

E-waste

Often waste that is illegal, too dangerous, or too expensive to dispose of safely or to recycle is dumped on other people—poor countries, poor people, and children. The best example of the United States and other developed countries trashing the country, futures, and lives of the poor of the developing world is e-waste. E-waste—electronic waste such as computers, cell phones, and televisions—is the fastest growing solid waste issue, as the amount is exponentially increasing and the waste itself contains toxic and hazardous chemical parts.

The United States alone throws away 130,000 computers per day.[9] In the United States, only 10 percent of e-waste is recycled. However, calling it recycling is misleading. Estimates are that 80 percent of the 300,000 to 400,000 tons of e-waste collected in the United States every year is shipped overseas to toxic waste dumps in countries such as Ghana, China, India, Pakistan, and Nigeria.[10] In these toxic e-waste dumps, people, many of them children, dismantle the e-waste for useful parts. Selling these bits of metal provides income to people in the slums. This process exposes them to a host of toxic chemicals, including PVC (polyvinyl chloride), PBB and PBOE (toxic flame retardants), lead, mercury, cadmium, and many others. (In Ghana, the locals living in the slum at the dump refer to the area as Sodom and Gomorrah.)[11] What remains after the burning and metal mining is dumped into waterways or fields or burned, which further exposes people in these countries to additional chemicals in the discarded e-waste materials.

The International Basel Convention has banned the transfer of e-waste from developed to developing countries, but the United States refuses to ratify this convention. In fact, of the 174 countries involved in the Basel Convention, Afghanistan, Haiti, and the United States are the only three that have not ratified the convention to ban toxic and hazardous waste transfer.[12] Waste trade is very profitable, and countries desperately in need of any source of income are not difficult to find. This may be one of the most blatant injustices that our country engages in related to solid waste disposal. The wealthy, waste-producing United States profits from dumping the toxic and hazardous remnants of our affluence onto the soils of the poor for their children to work with and live in.

Our waste creates a short-term profit for a few but risks the long-term health and well-being of the planet and the majority of people near waste sites. Affluence creates waste, but it is not the affluent who deal with this waste. As described elsewhere in this chapter, it is the poorest of the poor, those with the least, including children of all ages, who bear the burden of wasteful societies.[13]

Affluence creates waste. . . . It is the poorest of the poor . . . who bear the burden of wasteful societies.

Pollution Is Hell

All forms of waste disposal and pollution affect our environment, affecting first the Lazaruses of the world but then quickly the Diveses of the world, too. Pollution has health, economic, political, and many other effects, but it also creates environmental refugees. Bill McKibben encourages us to bridge the chasm by at least imagining for a moment how our lifestyle has influenced the Lazaruses who live in places where there are increasing environmental refugees:

> Computer models suggest that climate change will soon be creating hundreds of millions of refugees, fleeing rising waters or fields turned to desert (more refugees than we managed to create with all the bloody wars of the century we've just come through). . . . And then remembering that these people have done nothing to create the problem, that the 4 percent of the world living in America creates 25 percent of the carbon dioxide.[14]

To raise awareness about the real and imminent concern of people living on islands, the governmental cabinet of the Republic of Maldives, an atoll of islands in the Indian Ocean, held its meeting underwater in October 2009! President Mohammed Nasheed and his thirteen officials took their seats at twenty feet below the surface of the water in order to raise awareness of the reality that stokes their fear about the future of life in the country with the "lowest high" above sea level (seven feet, seven inches) in the world. Since the country expects to be flooded in the near future, the cabinet meeting included the signing of a document that called on all countries to cut their CO_2 emissions.[15]

An Inspiring Example

How would like to go to a church called Garbage Dump UMC?[16] That's essentially what Smokey Mountain United Methodist Church is called. The church is built next to the garbage dump in Manila, the capital city of the Philippines. The whole area is known as Smokey Mountain since it smolders from the fires. It could be called Lazarus United Methodist Church since it is home to the invisible and unimportant in the world's eyes, the victims of the marginalized in the Philippines. The dump was officially closed in the 1995 but its fires continue smoldering like Gehenna of old. It was closed not because it wasn't needed any more but because another site was opened nearby.

The Smokey Mountain United Methodist Church provides a kindergarten and nursery school for the children who live in the dump so that they can become educated. Their parents also receive literacy and skill training in order to provide them hope in a better life.

As Kathleen LaCamera says in her document, *Ministry to the Least of These*,

> Parents living on Smokey Mountain want their children to get an education, but have to spend all their time earning money for the fish and rice needed to survive. Scholarships have helped families buy the supplies and uniforms their children need to attend high school, which is tuition free. Some of the young people go on to college and professional training schools with the help of these scholarships.[17]

We bridge a bit of the chasm between Dives and Lazarus when we participate in providing for a ministry of mercy like that of Smokey Mountain United Methodist Church. But is mercy enough? What about justice ministries that could prevent the chasms that exist between us and people who live in such squalor?

A nearby Roman Catholic priest at Smokey Mountain works to broker deals with corporations and foreign governments to provide computer equipment for his own "scavenger congregation" so that they can find other ways of feeding their families. He works to minimize the negative impact created by discarded computer and high-tech gadgets, seeking solutions for both developing and wealthy nations regarding the recycling of electronic equipment.[18]

While children continue to be sacrificed in the garbage dumps of waste and refuse, we might think, *Well, while my garbage admittedly goes to some landfill somewhere, it's not going to these dumps where children live.* That's the problem with garbage. We put it out to be picked up and we think it's taken "away," but there is no "away." It ends up somewhere, and often somewhere involves someone who has to touch it, live in it, breathe it, or deal with it in some way.

It's the twenty-first century. Where is your old computer that you failed to properly recycle? Or even your properly recycled computer? Just because you sent it back to its maker or gave it to a recycling center doesn't ensure that it avoided landing in a dumping ground of e-waste.

Presently there is little regulation on the disposal of our equipment and on the U.S. export of electronic equipment. Therefore, up to 50 to 80 percent of e-waste collected by recyclers is not recycled but is cast away from our desks like bread scraps were cast away from Dives's table. Will we listen to the Law and the Prophets and someone risen from the dead to empower us to do justice for those who live like Lazarus?

Mottainai is a Japanese term that roughly translates to "what a waste." The ancient concept is based on Buddhist philosophy, meaning that one should never waste anything. Buddhists traditionally used the term to show regret for wasting anything sacred, such as religious lessons. In modern colloquial Japanese, *mottainai* is often heard if a child doesn't finish his rice or someone forgets to put the newspaper in the recycling bin. A neighbor will see and whisper "*mottainai*" under her breath.[19]

Sarah thinks that it would be a waste if we as Christians don't do what we can together to reduce pollution. It's a waste if we don't take action through mercy and justice. It's just a waste . . . of what Jesus has done for us.

Continuing the Journey—Do No Harm

Recall John Wesley's rules for living: do no harm, do good, and stay in love with God.

I began thinking about the connections between the three simple rules when I read a passage from the prophet Isaiah translated by Eugene Peterson in *THE MESSAGE*:

> I'm sick of your religion, religion, religion,
>> while you go right on sinning.
> When you put on your next prayer-performance,
>> I'll be looking the other way.
> No matter how long or loud or often you pray,
>> I'll not be listening.
> And do you know why? Because you've been tearing
>> people to pieces, and your hands are bloody.
> Go home and wash up.
>> Clean up your act.
> Sweep your lives clean of your evildoings
>> so I don't have to look at them any longer.
> Say no to wrong.
>> Learn to do good.
> Work for justice.
>> Help the down-and-out.
> Stand up for the homeless.
>> Go to bat for the defenseless. (Isaiah 1:14-17)

"Say no to wrong," as the prophet said, or "do no harm," as Wesley said, is a good place for each of us to start. Sarah and I are at very different points in our practices related to caring for the earth: she is alarmed and I'm concerned.[20] Our lives are vastly different. We have different living situations. We live in different parts of the country that affect where and how we get our food. We both lead full, active, and committed work lives, but they are very different. We recognize that one can't all of a sudden live totally in harmony with earth because that's nearly impossible given our culture's dependence on fossil fuels, agricultural practices, transportation systems, and other infrastructures based on nonsustainable practices.

Doing no harm, according to Wesley, included avoiding economic and social injustices such as "slaveholding," "buying or selling goods that have not paid the duty," "giving or taking things on usury—i.e., unlawful interest," "putting on of gold and costly apparel," "softness and needless self-indulgence," "laying up treasure upon earth," and "borrowing without a probability of paying; or taking up goods without a probability of paying for them."[21] Doing no harm has sharp dimensions cutting into many of our accepted lifestyles.

Doing no harm is a way of looking at any decision we make in terms of "if I do this, or more likely *don't* do this, eat this, drink this, or throw this away, then will I have prevented harm to the earth and the people who live upon it?"

A Commitment

Consider ways we as individuals, organizations, and countries do harm to developing nations and to helpless poor people.

CHAPTER 5
Take It to the Water

*If God loves the world, then how might any person of faith be
excused for not loving it or justified in destroying it?*
— **Wendell Berry** [1]

War of the Wells

Lack of water is a root cause of conflict in communities, countries,
and continents when it becomes a scarce resource. In Somalia, for
instance, two clans fought each other in what was called the War of the
Well, which was a conflict over a watering hole in the drought-stricken
town of Rabdore. After two years of fighting, 250 men from that town
were dead and there were "well widows, well warlords and well war-
riors."[2] Although we in the United States often hear of these conflicts
where communities fight each other, we fail to realize that they are
scarce-resource related.

The drought was affected by climate change, and when eleven
million people across East Africa suffered and lost their sources of
sustenance, such as water, livestock, and vegetation, violence broke
out. As one businessman in Somalia said, "Before I go anywhere in
Somalia, I pray. If someone is thirsty, they can shoot you for a glass

of water. There's no police to come and no government to say anything."[3]

My neighborhood, a suburb of Minneapolis, is home to hundreds of Somalis who have escaped because of the lack of food and water, and also because of the violence that environmental changes have caused, bringing them to a truly foreign climate of cold and snow. I'm aware that violence has made them refugees, but it's a water crisis that becomes a food crisis that becomes a war crisis that brings them to my neighborhood.

We take fresh, clean, available water for granted in most of our homes and communities across the United States. But that's not the case across the world, and even in some parts of the United States water is a scarce resource. Wherever water isn't available, there is conflict.

World Water Realities

The United Nations reported in 2005 that one in six people in the world lacked access to enough clean water to drink, wash, cook, and to use for sanitary purposes. The World Health Organization estimates that roughly three million people a year, mostly children under the age of five, die prematurely from drinking unsanitary water.[4] Every eight seconds a child dies of a waterborne illness.[5] As populations continue to swell and as poverty increases, the UN estimates that between two and seven billion people will face water shortages by 2050.[6]

People who use little more than a gallon per day may live in an area with polluted water, an area without a well to tap in to groundwater, an area where the number of people outstrip the nearby sources, or an urban area where the government lacks the funds and infrastructure to fix leaking pipes; provide clean, unpolluted water; and deliver consistent water service to homes.

According to UN data, in some countries women and girls walk an average of 3.7 miles a day carrying more than five gallons of water. In places in Africa, such as Kenya, it's more like six to twelve miles a day because of the drought and desertification that have occurred.[7] Because women and girls have to spend more and more time walking to find water as wells dry up, girls spend less time in school. Their formal education suffers, even though it is clear that the key factor in lifting communities out of poverty across the world is to educate girls.[8]

The whole community's future risks poverty when there's not clean, available water.

What if we interpret the familiar biblical story about the woman at the well from the perspective of women throughout the ages who lacked clean, available water and lived in hydrological poverty?

The Woman at the Well: Give Me Jesus

[Jesus] left Judea and started back to Galilee. But he had to go through Samaria. So he came to a Samaritan city called Sychar.... A Samaritan woman came to draw water, and Jesus said to her, "Give me a drink." (His disciples had gone to the city to buy food.) The Samaritan woman said to him, "How is it that you, a Jew, ask a drink of me, a woman of Samaria?" (Jews do not share things in common with Samaritans.) Jesus answered her, "If you knew the gift of God, and who it is that is saying to you, 'Give me a drink,' you would have asked him, and he would have given you living water." The woman said to him, "Sir, you have no bucket, and the well is deep. Where do you get that living water? Are you greater than our ancestor Jacob, who gave us the well, and with his sons and his flocks drank from it?" Jesus said to her, "Everyone who drinks of this water will be thirsty again, but those who drink of the water that I will give them will never be thirsty. The water that I will give will become in them a spring of water gushing up to eternal life." The woman said to him, "Sir, give me this water, so that I may never be thirsty or have to keep coming here to draw water." ... The woman said to him, "I know that Messiah is coming" (who is called Christ). "When he comes, he will proclaim all things to us." Jesus said to her, "I am he, the one who is speaking to you." ... Then the woman left her water jar and went back to the city. She said to the people, "Come and see a man who told me everything I have ever done! He cannot be the Messiah, can he?" They left the city and were on their way to him. (John 4:3-5a, 7-15, 25-26, 28-30)

Jesus went where people always went when they entered a town—to the well. The well was the gathering place. It's where people met others, and if there was a conflict, it would be at the well where travelers and worlds came together, clashed, or resolved their differences. When Moses went to the well, the women who had come to draw water were being harassed by some men, so he defended them (Exodus 2:15b-17). It was Jacob's well, a well-known and valued well in the history of the Jews *and* the Samaritans. In a sense, Jacob's well was as close to common ground as it came; both groups claimed and honored it.

Jesus sat down at the well and rested while his disciples went in search of food. Jesus had taken his disciples on the unpopular route that ran through Samaria, which was regarded as enemy territory, a place foreign and unfamiliar to them. Undoubtedly his disciples were uncomfortable and uncertain about why they were even there. The differences—and animosity—between the Jews and the Samaritans had to do with differing and conflicted histories, cultures, religions, and race.

While he was resting, Jesus encountered the women and girls who came to get water. The account never really says that there were *no* other women or girls at the well besides the "Samaritan woman." A number of women and girls might have been there, but he engaged in conversation with *one* of them.

He asked a woman for some water. The woman was taken aback, wondering why he as a Jew would ask her, as a Samaritan and a woman to boot, for a drink. Jesus' response to the woman's surprise was to say that if she knew who he was, she would be asking him for "living water." I always wonder what she was imagining. What did "living water" mean to her? Did she interpret it as something akin to running water, water available to her at all times so she wouldn't have to fetch it? Did she imagine water running into her home so she could open the tap and water would rush into her jar without her having to take a step outside? Water whenever she wanted it! Water, fresh, clean, and flowing—ever-flowing—into her home! She must have thought that this man was a dreamer because she found it hard to believe he had anything to do with living water since he didn't even have a bucket to draw a cup of it.

More on the Woman at the Well

Scholars suggest that the Samaritan woman was at the well at midday because she was a social outcast. But could there have been other reasons she was there in the heat of the day? Maybe her water jar tipped over and she needed to make the trek back to the well again. Maybe she feared the same things that women and girls fear today when they go to the well for water: that someone will hurt or harass them (like the men at the well where Moses rescued his future wife). As a result, she didn't want to go to the well before dawn or after dark because it was too risky. Maybe she had guests coming and she needed more water. Maybe she earned extra money by fetching someone else's water. Couldn't there be a few suggestions other than that she was an outcast, since the text itself doesn't bear this out?

If the fact that she had five husbands is what stigmatizes her as an outcast, could it be that she was subject to the levirate marriage law? That law held that if a woman's husband died before she had children to carry on the family name and heritage, she was to marry the husband's brother; and if he died, his next brother; and if he died, the next brother until she had a son (Deuteronomy 25:5-10). Although this isn't a law today for Jews or Christians, it is practiced in major areas of the world, including Asia and Africa. Both then and now, levirate marriage may be a lens into the story, explaining why she had five husbands.

Or, as some suggest, her "five husbands" were metaphoric. When the Assyrians conquered Israel, they removed the Jews and with them their religious traditions, but they brought Samaritans from five regions to replace them. The Samaritans from the five other regions came with their five gods and religions, although they continued to worship Yahweh. They were five nations of people "married" into one, and she was a part of their tradition. And the "husband" (or god) that she presently worshiped wasn't her real "husband" because she hadn't yet "married" herself to the living Christ who was sitting right in front of her, drinking a cup of water. Instead of being about an outcast woman, this story is about the relationship between God and non-Jews.[9]

Biblical have made much of the fact that the woman of Samaria went to the well in the middle of the day. Scholars have stated as fact that she was an outcast. As Jesus and the woman talked, the subject came up about her having had five husbands. This is the scholars' reason that she must have been an outcast. Why else would she be at yhe well in the heat of the day? This explanation is given almost every time this passage is read, taught, or preached.

Amy-Jill Levine suggests that the allusion to the woman being at the well at midday has more to do with the symbolism of light in the Gospel of John, where it is a metaphor for understanding and commitment to Jesus. Nicodemus visited Jesus in the middle of the night (John 3); he didn't fully embrace Jesus but stayed in the shadows of the story to the end. Mary Magdalene went "while it was still dark" (John 20:1) to the empty tomb, not yet understanding what she would come to understand in the full light of a new day. The woman at the well, however, "got it," as we say, and therefore the reference to midday suggests that she embraced Jesus and his everlasting water.[10]

The woman at the well became one of the first evangelists because Jesus established a relationship with her, begun by asking her to provide for his need. At first that seems almost chauvinistic, asking the woman to care for his needs. But most of us—men and women alike—are compassionate toward others when they demonstrate a need and ask for help. Most likely we will do whatever we can to assist them. Remember Jesus' words, "whoever gives even a cup of cold water to one of these little ones in the name of a disciple—truly I tell you, none of these will lose their reward" (Matthew 10:42). Giving water seems like a very important way of caring for others, and the woman at the well was willing to give water; in return she received so much more. She was doing what we as followers of Jesus are called to do! Would we do any less than give fresh, clean, and flowing water to those in need?

> The woman at the well was willing to give water; in return she received so much more. She was doing what we as followers of Jesus are called to do! Would we do any less than give fresh, clean, and flowing water to those in need?

Living Water: The Planet, Peace, and Poverty

The story of the woman at the well illustrates that water is often at the crucible of the planet, peace, and poverty. It is at the root of conflicts around the globe and will increasingly become central to conflict and violence. Water is an issue of the poor and a major key in ending poverty. It is essential in maintaining the balance of the ecosystem upon which we depend for so many goods and services. It is absolutely essential then that we face head-on the issues of water quality, distribution, access, sustainable use, and rights.

Water: The Planet

Water is at the center of the planet, peace, and poverty. It is a perfect example of how the other broad topics of life, our role on earth, resource use, and waste converge (food is another convergence point that we will explore in the next chapter).

The earth is often called the Blue Planet because it contains so much water. Remember from the rainforest examples in chapter 1 that water is an essential rule for having life. All life requires water! The human body itself is roughly 60 percent water. Unfortunately, 97 percent of earth's water is salt water, and 70 percent of fresh water is frozen in glaciers and ice caps. Water naturally cycles among the oceans, atmosphere, and land. For instance, our rainwater is evaporated ocean water that condenses over land masses. As water cycles, fresh water in lakes, rivers, streams, and underground aquifers is replenished, cleaned, and available to life forms, including humans.

Seventy percent of the water that humans use is for agriculture. It requires 33,100 gallons of water to produce 2.2 pounds of grass-fed beef. Twenty percent of our water use is for industrial purposes. Making one automobile requires 106,000 gallons of water. And 10 percent of our water use is for domestic and daily life purposes. Although we realize that we use water to shower, wash dishes and clothes, flush the toilet, and water the garden, we may not realize that many other activities also require water. On average, maintaining a golf course for one game requires 3,000 gallons of water. Golf courses require an enormous amount of fresh water to keep the greens green. Luckily work is under way to increase the efficiency of golf course watering.

Water: Peace

There is currently enough fresh water on earth to sustain life, but the water is not distributed equally, and even more important, water is not distributed according to human need. Canada has 0.05 percent of the world's population and roughly 20 percent of the world's available fresh water. Increasingly people move to warm and dry areas, but these areas do not have enough water for the people living there. The Los Angeles area has many more people than the water in L.A. can support, and so L.A. has been importing water from Northern California and the Colorado River to support the population and the surrounding agriculture.

Water is an issue of life and death. Humans can survive only a few days without water. Thus, water becomes an issue of health, economics, politics, government, and national and global security. Water is an issue of peace.

Conflicts over quantity, management, and sustainable use of water create rivals. The English word *rival* comes from a Latin term referring to the person with whom one shares the same stream or river. What if as water runs through three countries, the first country in the path diverts half of the water to irrigate its crops? What then if the second country builds a dam to provide power for its industries? What if there is little water left and what is left is heavily polluted by the time it reaches the third country? Although we associate war with differences based on religion and politics, wars based on sharing a scarce resource such as water are real. We hear about conflicts in the Middle East regarding to oil, but conflicts between rivals over water are just as historic and ongoing. Jordan, Syria, Palestine (Gaza and the West Bank), and Israel share water from the Jordan River; they're rivals, and there's conflict.

Water flows through Syria, then between the northern part of Jordan and Palestine, and finally between the southern part of Jordan and Israel. Potential conflict emerges as one country upstream uses more and more because of an increase in unchecked population while other countries downstream suffer from reduced amounts of water. The population of Syria is projected to nearly double between 2006 and 2050,[11] and this rise in population will correlate to an increased demand for water. To cope, Syria plans to build more dams and draw more water from the Jordan. The result will be a severe change in the amount of water available for Israel, Palestine, and Jordan farther downstream.

Since the Jordan River runs through Syria first, does Syria hold the right to do whatever it wants with the water? If so, it would be Syria's water to dam or store and use as the country pleases. Or is water a shared resource that no one owns? Do all countries have a right to the water that would flow through them if left unhindered? If this is the case, Jordan, Israel, and Palestine would be justified in feeling as if Syria is stealing some of their resource. If Syria has the rights to the water that flows through it, do Syrians have the right to bottle it and sell it to Jordan, Israel, and Palestine downstream?

The lack of access to water has been a problem between Palestinians in the Jordan Valley and Israel since Israel occupied the West Bank in 1967. Israel effectively denies Palestinians access to water to the extent that most Palestinians consume only about twenty liters a day while Israelis consume about three hundred liters.[12] The water usage is for irrigation of fruit and vegetables sold for export to Europe. The 450,000 Israelis living in West Bank settlements use as much or more water than the 2.3 million Palestinians in the same area.

In addition, the Jordan River has become so polluted near the Alumot Dam, which is a couple of miles south of the Sea of Galilee, with untreated and partially treated sewage, saline water, and fish pond effluents, that in addition to the stench, it is endangering the river to the point of extinction.[13] What responsibility does Israel have for the quality of the water?

There are 263 shared water basins around the world, only 158 have cooperative agreements.[14] We go to war for oil because we think we need oil. Water will be the next resource scarcity—and with a greater price because unlike oil there are no alternatives to water. It is said that if the twentieth century brought oil wars, the twenty-first century will bring water wars.

Issues of quality, accessibility, and cost of water create conflict around water rights. Is water a commodity that can be sold? Is there such a thing as water poverty or hydrological poverty? Who should own and manage water? Typically, governments own water and manage it as a public resource. However, more cities and even nations are turning over the management of their water to private companies. And with private management comes private ownership.

Water: Poverty

One in six people on earth lacks access to clean, safe drinking water. The lack of access to clean, safe water is an issue of poor people, but it is also an issue of women and children. In developing countries women typically fetch the water. Young girls drop out of school to help around the home and collect water. This has consequences when one considers that the development of countries, the decrease in birthrates, and the increasing wealth of nations correlate with the education of women and girls.

Without an option of clean water, the people of developing nations are forced to use whatever water is available. Often it is riddled with diseases. Each year three million people, mostly children under the age of five, die from waterborne diseases.

Poor nations, even those with water systems in place, face the reality that the availability of clean, safe water to all citizens requires money, technology, knowledge, and infrastructure. The municipal water systems of many nations are in dire need of repairs and upgrades. The situation is challenging and complex, however. Governments that have an interest in and accountability to their citizens lack funds, technology, knowledge, and infrastructure to make the necessary improvements to water sources for citizens. Private water companies, which continue to grow more powerful with time, have the funds, technology, knowledge, and infrastructural capacity to make real changes in water access and water quality around the world. They also have an increasing desire to do this. Water companies, the three largest in particular, are working to buy as many water sources as possible around the world. Privatizing municipal water sources in the United States and around the world is becoming the norm.

While private control promises improvements in water access and quality, it comes at an often enormous cost to the poor people of our world. Private companies have the ability to do what governments of poor nations do not, but private companies do not serve, have an interest in, or have accountability to the people in nations that need the water. Private companies serve, have an interest in, and are accountable to their shareholders. This is the crux of the water privatization issue. The poor cannot afford water. They can barely afford the scraps of food that they eat and the meager roof over their heads. Water companies are interested in people who can pay for water; they are not interested in providing clean water for the poor at little or no charge. Think about it. If you were a shareholder in a water company and your stock didn't move, but you got a report that South Africa was now providing clean water to all the citizens, even the poorest, in the country, would that be ok? Even if it feels good, people don't buy stocks for philanthropic reasons; they buy stocks to make money, to make an investment in their future. There is an inherent conflict of interest between the needs of poor nations and private water companies, but this trend is encouraged and even forced to an extent by the World Bank and corruptive or easily bribed government officials.

Three European water companies—Suez, Vivendi or Veolia (different names but same company), and RWE/Thames (which has a host of other names as well)—aim to control as much of the world's private and publicly owned water as possible.[15] In general, privatization encourages selling water as opposed to conserving it and does not address the inability of the poor to pay for water in the first place. Many believe the result is turning a public good over to the private hands of corporations.

The motives of these multinational corporations are further complicated by their ties to the World Bank. The World Bank is designed to provide financial stability and development opportunities to developing countries. It is financed by richer nations with the intent of developing poor nations. However, the World Bank often offers debt relief to nations in exchange for privatizing their water through one of these main water companies. Examples include Buenos Aires, Argentina (Suez); Puerto Rico (Veolia); Djakarta, Indonesia (RWE/Thames); and Santiago, Chile (Veolia).[16] In addition, government officials are often bribed or given generous gifts as incentives to privatize otherwise public water sources.[17]

Beyond privatizing water, the World Bank encourages the indirect export of water as an exchange for debt relief. For instance, the World Bank supports Kenya's intensive rose industry. Roses are grown in Kenya and shipped to Europe. To grow a dozen roses requires just over thirty gallons of water. To grow roses in a water-poor country is insane. It is simply for profit of the rich on the backs of the poor, and the practice has been called theft and murder.[18] Regardless, in these cases, development aid from the World Bank ends up being financial investments for rich and powerful water companies.

Citizens who are promised increased access to water following privatization often find locked, metered taps where they once had free-flowing water. For example, in countries such as Ghana and South Africa, new wells are created or existing wells are taken over, and the private companies lock the flow of water and charge extremely high fees for use. In Ghana, water flows irregularly and unpredictably from taps, but people are charged even for the air that flows when a tap is opened and no water flows out. In South Africa, a meter is locked onto the well's tap, customers pay for an electronic key that turns on the water, and extremely expensive water flows out. Often people cannot afford the new, clean, privatized water that is available and so they choose to return to the streams of free water that contain waterborne diseases, such as cholera.[19]

The question is, is water a human right or a marketable commodity? If it is a human right, how do we pay for clean, safe water to be available to poor people? If it is a marketable commodity, how do we ensure that poor people have access to water? What would Jesus' response to our water crises be?

Christians, specifically United Methodist groups, raise money to dig wells, which are given to communities at no cost. A well is sometimes the beginning of a new church in places like the Congo. People need clean water; a well is given to the village so their women and girls don't have to walk so far; and when it's given without cost, their response is: give me Jesus! It is a witness to the life-giving power of God's love. Especially in light of how people in conditions of drought, poverty, and poverty-related diseases are denied free access to their own water, water is life and life is Jesus. To care for our neighbor is to make sure that others have clean, fresh, and available water.

The Journey of the Bottle of Water

Go on another journey of a familiar object: the journey of the water bottle. One of the most common misuses of water in our American lifestyle is the prevalent use of bottled water, especially when there is *no health reason* to use bottled water.

Over the last decade bottled water has become a mainstay for many Americans as well as people around the globe. While one out of six people in the world doesn't have dependable, safe drinking water, most people in the United States don't need their water from a bottle in order to ensure its safety or purity. Bottled water is a marketing phenomenon, especially in the United States, creating a need where there was no need.

The story is fascinating in and of itself, but one of the real scams of bottled water is that it is advertised as being healthier than tap water for most Americans. Municipal water is tested regularly in cities across the country, but the water that goes into the bottles is far less regularly tested. We don't really know the quality of water in the bottle we purchased. And unlike those for tap water, the public does not have legal access to test records. Bottled water is an expensive convenience, even a luxury.

While one out of six people in the world doesn't have dependable, safe drinking water, most people in the United States don't need their water from a bottle in order to ensure its safety or purity.

Bottled water is a consumer of resources. If we paid for our municipal water at the rate we pay for bottled water, most of our *monthly* water bills would be about $9,000.[20] When it comes to stewardship of our financial resources, drinking bottled water is not a good choice. Granted, if we choose water instead of a sugary drink, it is healthier—but not healthier than a bottle of water that we have filled from our water tap or better than water we've placed in our own reusable container and placed in the refrigerator to use when we're thirsty or to take with us on a trip.

The plastic bottles also have a big carbon footprint. Bottled water is heavy, weighing eight and a third pounds per gallon. An eighteen-wheeler can't be filled with bottled water alone; it must have empty space or be filled with other commodities because a truck full of bottled water would be too heavy to pull. Yet the United States ships one billion bottles of water a week via ships, trains, and trucks.[21] It wouldn't take too many bottles of water to equal the amount of fossil fuel used to drive a large SUV! Even glass bottles that are reused by some companies require up to twice as much water to clean as what they hold. Some bottled-water–producing companies put the tap water through an extra energy-intensive filtration system to ensure that the water from one municipal area tastes the same; then they can "brag about the purity" no matter where the water is bottled.[22]

Furthermore, the bottles are a major pollution problem when it comes to their disposal. "We pitch into landfills 38 billion water bottles a year—in excess of $1 billion worth of plastic," according to some accounts.[23] While the water bottles are recyclable, we only recycle less than 20 percent of them and the rest are pitched into landfills.

Bottled water for Americans is simply a convenience that consumes more resources than is justifiable in most situations. It's consumerism at its worst. As American consumers we should be outraged at how we have been duped into thinking that we need bottled water and therefore spend the exorbitant amount of money that we do on it.

> When a whole industry grows up around supplying us with something we don't need—when a whole industry is built on the packaging and presentation—it's worth asking how that happened, and what the impact is. And if you do ask, if you trace both the water and the business back to where they came from, you find a story more complicated, more bemusing, and ultimately more sobering than the bottles we tote everywhere suggest.[24]

As Christians when we think about how precious water is as a resource and how it represents life to so many in our world, we should think twice about consuming a cold bottle of water just because it's there, ready and available to us.

Will I never drink water from a plastic bottle again? I probably will when I have no other alternative, such as when I'm in a country where the water would make me sick. We must always recycle the bottles. But often people choose bottled water in their travel and at home when there's the possibility for cold water other than from a bottle.

One pastor challenged members of his congregation to put aside one dollar every time they drank bottled water. If they were given or asked for a glass of water in a restaurant and didn't drink it, they were to put aside one dollar. They collected the money and used it to purchase a well in Africa. Again, it's a way to become more mindful of our misuse of the water that we consume at a high expense to ourselves and at the expense of others.

What Does This Have to Do with Us as Followers of Jesus?

The story of the woman at the well reminds us that as followers of Jesus, we have received the life-giving waters of baptism. The baptismal liturgy recalls the ways in which God has saved God's people throughout our salvation history through water. We remember in the Thanksgiving Prayer over the Water that God has saved people through the ark, brought people out of Egypt through the sea into freedom, "and sent Jesus, nurtured in the water of a womb," to save God's people.

Following the Thanksgiving Prayer over the Water, we say the vows, forgetting sometimes that the vows of baptism *begin* with the renunciation of sin, preceding the profession of faith in Jesus Christ. So before the water comes upon us in baptism, we promise to "renounce the spiritual forces of wickedness, reject the evil powers of this world, and repent of [our] sin."

What does it mean to "renounce the spiritual forces of wickedness... [and] evil powers"? To begin with, it means that we renounce those forces in our world that keep women and girls subject to the lack of fresh, clean, accessible water, denying them education and an opportunity for a future outside poverty. There are ways through our acts of mercy and justice that can provide for others around the world; our renunciation of wickedness and evil may have to do with our own apathy and lack of concern!

The second vow of baptism is: "Do you accept the freedom and power God gives you to resist evil, injustice, and oppression in whatever forms they present themselves?" Evil, injustice, and oppression have many manifestations, and those manifestations may be within us as well as within the "powers and principalities" of the world. When we learn that worldwide there are one billion people without clean, accessible water and that three thousand children a day die from unclean water,[25] we must renounce the evil and injustice that allow this to happen, and we must repent of our sin of complicity, silence, and resistance to act on their behalf. We are called as Christians to resist such things as participating in corporations and conveniences that perpetuate the injustice and hardship of others. We may have to make a sacrifice, something as simple and yet as profound as resisting the temptation to drink bottled water.

Both vows have to do with facing evil and injustice in our world, having the will to make the renunciation of wickedness and our own sins of commission and omission in relation to what it means to be a follower of Jesus primary in our discipleship. Will we have this will to resist evil and to do justice?

Then we are asked if we profess Jesus Christ as our Savior, put our trust in his grace, and promise to serve him. One might expect that the vows of baptism would *begin* with a profession of faith in Jesus Christ, and then as a result of our confession, we would renounce evil and accept the freedom and power God gives us to resist evil, injustice, and oppression. However, the vows of baptism aren't separate or linear but comprehensive of what a Christian life is meant to be. Rejecting evil and resisting injustice are part of putting our trust in Jesus and promising to serve him in our daily lives. Unless we reject evil and resist injustice, we'll never fully understand what it means to put our trust in God's grace.

> The vows of baptism call us to "sit at the wells of life" with others who need the basics of life, such as clean, accessible water.

The vows of baptism call us to "sit at the wells of life" with others who need the basics of life, such as clean, accessible water. They need Jesus, but first they need for us to face the injustices and evil in our world that deny them their basic needs and rights to water.

When people ask why we would speak out against the injustices of climate change and the lifestyle that produces it in our world, it is through none other than our vows of baptism. In fact, we have no choice! We promised to speak out and take steps toward caring for the earth when we took the vows of baptism or confirmed our vows of baptism. That's what it means to be marked by the waters of baptism.

An Inspiring Example

A couple of years ago, Justin Oelschlager, a young teenager at the time, started attending a new worship service at his church, The Well. He and his family enjoyed it and became regular attenders at its services. Justin heard about the need for wells in villages in other countries. He learned that children in other countries often have to walk a long way to get water. As a result, the children, especially the girls, often miss school.

Justin thought his worshiping community, The Well, could provide a well so a village would have its basic need of water. He became a primary fund-raiser for the well project. The connections between what he was learning and experiencing in worship caused him to think about how to help others. In many ways, Justin's life was totally disconnected from the experience of being without clean, accessible water, having to carry water, and missing school as a result, but it captured his imagination and it compelled him to do something about the need that led him to raise the money as well as the awareness of something as basic as water.

A little over a year later, a small village in Sierra Leone was the recipient of his efforts. Justin is ecstatic at the difference he has been able to make with the help of his worshiping community. The well project not only changes lives in Sierra Leone; it has already changed Justin's life, made his world larger, and broadened the experience of others at The Well, too. His life and others at The Well in Roseville, Minnesota, have had Jesus and water seamlessly connected in their hearts and minds.

Justin may not be able to articulate it, but he has definitely incorporated the theology of baptism into his life. Baptized in Christ, he was inspired and empowered by the Spirit and a faith community to address the injustices associated with water in our world and to make a difference. In fact, Justin demonstrates how sometimes we come to faith, or a deepened faith, because we face the world's injustices and do something about them.

Continuing the Journey—Do Good

Learning to do good is part of discipleship. A *disciple* is someone who is a student. Learning to do good is growing in our knowledge and wisdom in living according to the ways of Jesus and consistent with the ancient biblical traditions of community, health, and the importance of the earth. Part of discipleship is peacemaking, and by learning to do good we are also being peacemakers as we draw closer to the people around us and become more aware and concerned about our neighbors far away and in the future as they seek to live on this earth.

Learning to do good might also involve learning more about policies, beginning in one's community as well as nation. Those of us who live in cities might not think about the amount of water we consume.

When Sarah and I talk with others about Jesus and the environment, sometimes people want to point fingers at others who aren't doing as much as they're doing with recycling, living simply, using responsible transportation, composting, consuming, and so on. There's no room for blame but instead mutual learning to do good, one with another and in support of one another.

When Jesus spoke to the woman at the well, he asked her for a drink, and in return he gave her living water. Our neighbors are dying of thirst, and our consumption practices are in need of improvement. Let us together learn to do good by paying attention to our baptism call to "sit at the wells of life" with our brothers and sisters.

A Commitment

Think about the water you consume each week. Remember your baptism; honor and enjoy the availability of clean water. Find a way to participate in providing clean water, either through your habits or through your efforts with others—United Methodist Committee on Relief (www.UMCOR.org), Blood: Water Mission (www.bloodwatermission.com), or Ginghamsburg Church's Miracle Offering (www.theSudanProject.org), for example—to be a part of clean water initiatives.

CHAPTER 6
Bless This Food!

Unless someone like you cares a whole lot, nothing is going to get better. It's not.

— The Once-Ler, from Dr. Seuss's eco-children's classic, *The Lorax*

A café in Philadelphia called the White Dog Café began as a humble take-out coffee and muffin shop on the first floor of a house. The menu grew and with it the use of the house. Soon the café expanded to operate out of the second floor and also the basement and the backyard. Renovations and expansions made it a widely known restaurant in the Philadelphia area. It had truly expanded to meet a large market of interested people. Good food, good marketing, and a good business plan helped Judy Wicks with a small but successful business, resulting in a food and culture program with a core group of her customers and employees called "Table for 6 Billion, Please!"[1]

People connect all over the world—Nicaragua, Russia, Vietnam, Lithuania, Israel, Palestine, and more—and adopt a sister restaurant. Through their food connection with others who are also interested in food and eating, who want to establish more sustainable ways of providing and acquiring food, and who believe that we understand one another better from what we hold in common, an international community is built around food.

The idea is that when we sit down at the table with strangers, we make the table a bigger place—and the world a smaller place. What if food brought us together as Christians, and when we sat together at table—the open table of the Lord's Supper as well as our potluck tables and our own kitchen tables—we found community?

And God Said, "Let There Be Food!"

After God created creatures and humanity on the sixth day, God provided food for all living beings.

> God said, "See, I have given you every plant yielding seed that is upon the face of all the earth, and every tree with seed in its fruit; you shall have them for food. And to every beast of the earth, and to every bird of the air, and to everything that creeps on the earth, everything that has the breath of life, I have given every green plant for food." And it was so. God saw everything that he had made, and indeed, it was very good. (Genesis 1:29-31a)

God's provision of food is a crowning gift for all created beings, including humanity. It's almost as if we read the sixth day of creation and are so excited to see ourselves in the story that we forget the providence of God: the seed-bearing plants that provide food for all living creatures. If there is a pinnacle to the creation story, my friends, it looks to me like it's food!

But after God gave the crowning gift of food, food became the source that caused the fall of humanity and foreclosure on the Garden of Eden for Adam and Eve. God told them not to eat of the tree that was in the middle of the garden, but they ate the food explicitly forbidden to them: "So when the woman saw that the tree was good for food, and that it was a delight to the eyes, and that the tree was to be desired to make one wise, she took of its fruit and ate; and she also gave some to her husband, who was with her, and he ate" (Genesis 3:6).

When God discovered that Eve took the forbidden food, gave it to Adam, and both consumed what was not theirs to consume, the first food fight broke out. Animosity and blame replaced the previous harmony that existed between them. Ashamed of themselves, Adam and Eve hid from the presence of God, and when God asked Adam if he had eaten the forbidden food, Adam replied by saying, "The woman whom you gave to be with me, she gave me the fruit from the tree, and I ate" (Genesis 3:12), blaming Eve. When God asked the woman what happened, she said that the serpent tricked her and she ate. We often humorously think of this response as something akin to "the devil made me do it," but in fact they were tempted to "be like God" (Genesis 3:5). Hubris or pride made them want what wasn't theirs to have, and their overconsumption forced them out of Eden and consigned them to toil, suffering, and enmity between them. In addition, their relationship with the other creatures was disrupted as the verdict was pronounced against the serpent: "cursed . . . among all animals" (Genesis 3:14).

Breaking the one (food) rule that God gave them caused broken relationships between them, between them and God, between them and other creatures, and between them and the land itself as they were exiled to "thorns and thistles" (Genesis 3:18) instead of having the pick of all the seed-bearing plants of the Garden of Eden. The goodness and joy of God's provision of food were spoiled like rotting fruit on a hot summer's day. So much for being usufructuaries!

And we find ourselves today among the series of broken relationships. Our overconsumption and poor stewardship of food create animosity and disharmony with other people and creatures. Once again we discover that the scarcity of food—often by how it is produced, distributed, and consumed—causes violence. We keep falling into sin—but Jesus comes to the rescue!

Jesus' Followers Feed Everyone!

From the youngest child to the oldest person, most people know the story about the loaves and the fish. Jesus provided for the people, just as God provided for humanity's need for food. But it's also a story about how God restores our broken relationships with God, with others, and with creation itself, giving us a model for living based on the

Eucharist. The feeding of the five thousand is like a redemptive reversal of the story of the Fall: from scarcity to abundance; from individuals to community; from local to global. In this story about Jesus, we find a joyful and just way to eat.

Eating on Earth as in Heaven

The day was drawing to a close, and the twelve came to him and said, "Send the crowd away, so that they may go into the surrounding villages and countryside, to lodge and get provisions; for we are here in a deserted place." But he said to them, "You give them something to eat." They said, "We have no more than five loaves and two fish—unless we are to go and buy food for all these people." For there were about five thousand men. And he said to his disciples, "Make them sit down in groups of about fifty each." They did so and made them all sit down. And taking the five loaves and the two fish, he looked up to heaven, and blessed and broke them, and gave them to the disciples to set before the crowd. And all ate and were filled. What was left over was gathered up, twelve baskets of broken pieces. (Luke 9:12-17)

Although Jesus told his disciples not to worry about what to eat or drink (Luke 12:22), here and other places throughout the Gospels, he demonstrated that he cared deeply that people were hungry. Hunger is a symbolic sign of sin—not the sin of the one who is hungry, but the sin of humanity as a sign that we're not in right relationship with one another, God, and earth itself, and thereby people go without food.

Why were the people hungry? They weren't hungry just because they spent the day out on the hillsides listening to Jesus and (*a*) they forgot their lunch, (*b*) there were no fast-food places to pick something up, or (*c*) they simply missed a single meal. The people were hungry because they experienced poverty and hunger on a regular basis. Most of the people who followed Jesus suffered from food insecurity or scarcity much of the time.

But why would people living along a lake full of fish and hills waving with grain be hungry? When agriculture is working in a biblical and environmentally just way, the city and countryside live in a symbiotic relationship with each other; they need each other. There is plenty for the farmer as well as the city that needs the produce and fish. The Roman Empire exacted heavy taxes and extracted the bounty from the land, for the purpose of supporting its military regime, at the expense of the peasants who farmed the land and fished the sea. Even the temple in Jerusalem exploited the peasants with heavy tithes to support its building and operations. As a result, people on the land and sea who should have had enough were poor and suffered food insecurity.

Often we think major global issues like hunger and poverty are unsolvable because they overwhelm us, but solutions begin with one or two here and there, working together for the common good, changing habits, asking different questions, and doing new things.

The disciples went to Jesus, asking him to dismiss the crowds because the people were hungry. Jesus had a more excellent way of dealing with the hunger of the crowds. He told the disciples to feed them. The disciples understandably objected! The request was too great; they could never find the resources to provide food for such a crowd. Jesus knew that no one had the individual means to feed the whole group of five thousand (plus women and children, according to the story in Matthew 14:13-21) but wanted to see how the disciples would care for people's needs.

The Gospel of John (6:9) states that a young boy brought the first gift of five loaves and two fish. It usually just takes one to get a miracle started; as Gandhi said, "If you want to see change, be the change you want to see." The power of one began to eliminate the hunger of the crowds. Often we think major global issues like hunger and poverty are unsolvable because they overwhelm us, but solutions begin with one or two here and there, working together for the common good, changing habits, asking different questions, and doing new things.

Starting with the power of this one boy to produce five loaves and two fish, Jesus instructed his disciples to put people in groups of fifty. I've always wondered about the importance of this instruction. Some scholars believe that it mirrors Moses when he grouped people in order to resolve matters between them, placing leaders over small groups to solve their problems (Exodus 18:13-23). Is the grouping of the five thousand (plus women and children) a symbol of the Exodus experience that reminds us that when we're in community with one another, we are better able to resolve our differences?

Once the people were in groups of fifty, Jesus took what they had and turned toward heaven to bless the loaves and fish. When they sat down in small groups the masses of the crowd became the faces of people and families that they knew or quickly came to know. When we face our neighbors we are more likely to reach into our pockets and purses and dig out a little more, enough here and there to make a difference for the whole group. Folk might have forked over their little bit of food, put it together, and fed the group of fifty. And the group next to them fed their group of fifty. And on and on it went. Working locally (groups of fifty) solved the global problem (a group of five thousand plus women and children). Jesus restored the brokenness of eating in the Garden of Eden by putting people together in community so that there was enough—more than enough—for everyone.

Could those groups of fifty be reflective of restoring community locally in order to solve global or really big problems, such as world hunger and poverty? When each person within the community works together with others, there's enough for all. Not only enough for all, but leftovers. Jesus demonstrated a different economy—God's economy of abundance—in contrast to an economy of scarcity generated by the Roman Empire where some had plenty and others had none.

Why would we consider it a miracle only if Jesus prayed and the heavens rained down bread and fish for the crowds? A miracle seems to have more to do with the outcome than the process. Did God have a role in the miracle if it happened like that? Yes, a miracle occurs when everyone who has something provides what he or she has so that everyone has enough. *Enough*: a simple word that means a sufficient amount, not too much and not too little, but just right. With "just eating" there's enough for everyone.

Jesus blessed the food that the crowd was to partake because it came from an economy of abundance instead of scarcity. How blessed is our food? We can romanticize the planting, tending, harvesting, preserving, cooking, and eating food that we have grown or we receive from friends and family with gardens. Yet the food as it is grown, harvested, transported, processed, cooked, and the form in which we eat it is not always healthy, much less holy. We may say a perfunctory prayer over our food, but what does it mean to truly ask God's blessings upon it? If food has arrived on our table or we eat it in a fashion that brings injustice and even bloodshed, disease, poverty, violence, or warfare to others, how can our food be blessed?

Ellen Davis describes blessing for us: "Blessing is essentially the transformative experience of knowing and honoring God as the Giver; it means valuing the steady flow that sustains the world even above the gift of life that each of us receives and is in time constrained to relinquish."[2]

When Jesus blessed the food, he acknowledged God as the giver and each of us in a right relationship with God and one another so that we might live in God's economy of abundance as God created it in Eden.

The story of the loaves and fish reminds us of the words of our other sacrament, the Lord's Supper or Eucharist. The Last Supper was a very special meal that Jesus shared with his disciples as a Passover meal before his death and resurrection. With the traditional Passover meal come many blessings over the food; it's blessed again and again.

> When the hour came, he took his place at the table, and the apostles with him.... Then he took a loaf of bread, and when he had given thanks, he broke it and gave it to them, saying, "This is my body, which is given for you. Do this in remembrance of me." And he did the same with the cup after supper, saying, "This cup that is poured out for you is the new covenant in my blood." (Luke 22:14, 19-20)

Jesus restores people to proper relationships through these words in both the story of the feeding of the five thousand and the Prayer of Thanksgiving: he took bread (food), blessed it, and gave it to his disciples. If Jesus came to restore and reconcile the brokenness we have with others, the earth itself, and God, then Jesus expects his followers to take the food we have and be the miracle we say we want to be. Later the Christian church was concerned about this same dynamic at the Lord's Table as occurred out on the hillside of Galilee: some came to eat with more than they needed, and others had nothing (1 Corinthians 11:17-22). Jesus' blessing calls us to see one another and our neighbors with the love and respect to make sure that all our tables and the food we share with one another is blessed, holy, and healthy for those who produce it as well as those who eat it.

If we fail to live in the economy of abundance, just as in the Garden of Eden and even at the Last Supper, conflict will prevail. All was not well that night at dinner; Jesus' disciples were fighting about who was greatest among them. We like to think that the Last Supper was peaceful, serene, and calm, so it might surprise us that there was fighting. Jesus said to his disciples in the midst of their conflict:

> The kings of the Gentiles lord it over them; and those in authority over them are called benefactors. But not so with you; rather the greatest among you must become like the youngest, and the leader like one who serves. (Luke 22:25-26)

"Not the way it will be with you" were Jesus' words to his disciples. We are called to act differently, especially at the table, from the rest of the culture around us. "Not the way it will be with you": we are to be people who care about the ways in which others are exploited in the production of our food. "Not the way it will be with you": we are to care that there's not enough for others and that food scarcity causes violence in our world.

When Jesus said, "Do this in memory of me," he meant that we are to repeat the patterns of sharing in God's economy with our neighbors, making sure that all our food is blessed—at our Communion table, our potluck tables, our kitchen tables, and the tables of those who live in food scarcity. Like the story of the feeding of the five thousand, we are reminded of the sacrament—the outward and visible sign of the inward and invisible grace—that is food.

Jesus Took the Food...

"The five loaves and the two fish..." What do we call food today? Filling the grocery shelves, our kitchen pantries, and our dinner tables is stuff that we have come to think of as food but is actually food mixed, processed, and prepared into a chemical, food-related pile of stuff.

Sarah jokes with her students about their peanut butter. "What are the ingredients of peanut butter?" she asks. One would think peanuts and salt, but more often than not there is a whole paragraph worth of ingredients. The same is true for most of the packaged food we eat. What if we just bought whole foods, meaning food in its original form? Then what if we ate or cooked with only whole foods? Think how different it would be: meals from scratch. It would mean shopping and cooking like our grandmothers used to do. Remember grandmas who made their own jam or bread or spaghetti sauce?

Sarah suggested to her students that their generation will be the last to remember how grandmas used to cook or bake. Their children will have grandmothers in the generation of microwaves and packaged and reheated dinners. It's odd what we have come to accept as our food.

Jesus Blessed the Food...

Would Jesus bless the food on our tables? Just as our stuff has stories, so does the food we eat. When we sit down to a table of food, we often fail to realize that the system that produces our food is filled with injustices and unethical practices.

Farmers who produce our food struggle economically. In addition, 70 percent of the corn, 80 percent of the soy, and 33 percent of our marine catch are used to feed factory-farmed or feedlot animals. These animals are raised, transported, and slaughtered using inhumane conditions and practices that breed disease, pollute the air and water, and risk the well-being of humans at various steps in the process. Eighteen percent of greenhouse gas emissions come from meat production. The animals we eat produce more than twenty times the waste that humans in our country do, but there is no sewage system in place to deal with the waste, allowing it to pollute our waterways.

The system of food production relies on 2.4 million pounds of pesticides per year in the United States alone, and this figure does not take into account the chemicals added to animal feed, the steroids or antibiotics pumped into animals, and the chemicals added to packaged food in processing. The system of our food production uses ten times more energy, in the forms of fossil fuel energy primarily, to produce the food than it provides to the people eating it! In other words, it takes ten units of fossil fuel energy to put one unit of food energy on the table.

Remember from chapters 1 and 2 that rich genetic and species diversity creates a strong, stable fabric of life. The decrease in plant and animal genetic diversity puts all of us at risk as conditions on our planet change and as new diseases emerge. Our industrialized food industry has selected only a small number of genetic strains of plants and breeds of animals for our food.

Aldo Leopold, an environmental ethicist, once said, "There are two spiritual dangers in not owning a farm. One is the danger of supposing that breakfast comes from the grocery, and the other that heat comes from the furnace."[3] So much of what we eat is so modified, processed, and packaged that it bears little or no resemblance to anything grown, raised, or caught in the natural world. Much of what we assume to be true about food, including where it comes from, how it is produced, and even how good it is for us, is not the case at all. The vast majority of the food we eat is produced with processes that cause great harm to our bodies, our planet, and our spirits. Being unaware of these processes that bring our food to the table is dangerous, and as Aldo Leopold warned, it is a spiritual danger as much as a health or environmental one.

> "There are two spiritual dangers in not owning a farm. One is the danger of supposing that breakfast comes from the grocery, and the other that heat comes from the furnace."—Aldo Leopold

The food produced in the United States increased dramatically during the 1950s and 1960s thanks to technology, but this increase came at a price. Agriculture is the world's largest industry, and in the United States, agribusiness, which includes growing, processing, distributing, and selling food, is larger than the automotive, steel, and housing industries combined.[4]

This business is also the most environmentally harmful industry. The production of our food, originating from rangelands, oceans or fisheries, and cropland, pollutes the water and air, destroys the land's topsoil, and consumes natural water and energy resources.

The question is, why are we producing food this way? Is this the only way we can feed ourselves, or is this one of many options? What reasons are there to choose to produce food in a manner that is so dangerous to our planet, our spirits, and ourselves? Why have we moved away from a process of being in touch with, in connection with, and in partnership with the planet and toward one of mass producing as much food as possible with minimal regard for the planet and life involved? Our agribusiness production has put us once again outside the Garden of Eden.

Prior to the 1950s, food was produced by a large number of farmers who grew a variety of crops. Farmers strategically planted different crops and rotated them so that the soil could rejuvenate. Farmers were in touch with the seasons, the resident bugs, the seeds, the soil, and the crops. They understood, paid close attention to, and relied on a balanced but dynamic system around them.

This way of growing food is called traditional farming. It involves individuals or a family farm that practices on a smaller scale (albeit much larger than a backyard vegetable garden) with multiple species, without the use of chemicals, and within the larger natural system. The food is grown for the local community or surrounding areas.

Traditional farming ended as World War II ended. The system of producing food has moved from traditional, family-owned farms in connection with a natural system to an industrialized, corporately controlled, disconnected, and largely broken system. The industrialized food system is geared to maximize efficiency and profit, and that narrow focus on efficiency and profit has brought risks and costs. There have been drastic increases in the use of fossil fuels, water, synthetic fertilizers, and chemical pesticides. Industrial agriculture, which now accounts for four-fifths of the world's food production, uses enormous greenhouses, encourages growing a single crop on cropland (monocultures), and raises livestock and food animals in feedlots and food factories or factory farms.[5] Would Jesus bless food that uses large amounts of energy and water, produces large amounts of animal waste and other pollution, and decreases biodiversity?

Our Daily Bread

Sarah recently watched the food documentary *Our Daily Bread*[6] with a seven- and an eight-year-old, Ryan and Jake, as she prepped for films to show in her environmental science class for the upcoming school year.[7] *Our Daily Bread* is fascinating in what it teaches, but even more in how it conveys its message. The entire movie lacks narration, explanation, and words. The viewer relies completely on what he or she sees and hears during the process of various aspects of food production, including the production of apples, tomatoes, eggs, chicken, pork, beef, milk, fish, and many other foods. Throughout the movie, the viewer hears the constant and eventually haunting sound of machines.

Machines are the most constant part of the process of food production. Machines feed the animals, transport the animals, water the crops, sort the produce, pick up the chickens, move the animals to slaughter, and perform many other steps. As we watched the movie—and it held the attention of the seven- and eight-year-old as much as it held mine—I grew concerned. Was this appropriate for children? The boys had questions about what was happening, and as children do, they had a series of follow-up *whys*.

Jake: What are they doing?
Sarah: They're debeaking the chicks.
Jake: Why?
Sarah: Because they are kept in such tight quarters that they will peck one another to death if they have their sharp beaks.
Ryan: That must hurt.
Sarah: I'm sure it does, but they aren't like chickens that can run all around and have their own space.
Jake: Why don't they just let them outside and give them more space?
Ryan: Or they could have fewer chickens so they could have more room.

It's not easy for children to understand that profit drops significantly as the space per chicken increases. The industrial process that Jake, Ryan, and I watched maximized efficiency and profit, and that is how the roughly nine billion broiler or meat chickens are raised in this country.[8]

Surprises in the food production occurred again and again, raising questions for both Sarah and the inquiring young boys. A scene that appeared more like a sterile morgue or perhaps an area where scientists were storing secret technology turned out to be enormous incubators for eggs. During the course of an hour and a half, Sarah and the children's thoughts and comments moved from confused and questioning to disturbed, upsetting, and sickening. The way we raise, feed, and slaughter the meat we eat feels wrong to watch.

The process of large-scale or industrialized egg, milk, and meat production begs the question, "Can we bless this food?" when, for instance, 280 million egg-laying hens in the United States are in such small "battery" cages and packed so tightly that they can neither stand up nor spread their wings.[9] Each of the five to eight birds in the fourteen-square-inch cage has been debeaked and is exposed to nearly constant light to increase egg production. The nine billion broiler chickens, raised for meat, have been so genetically altered that their legs and internal organs often cannot support their enormous breasts, now seven times heavier than they were twenty-five years ago.[10] These chickens live in such tightly packed conditions and spend so much time in their own waste (usually lying down because they cannot support their own weight) that they must be given four times the antibiotics used for humans and cows combined.[11] With no laws to protect the raising, transporting, and slaughtering of chickens, it is possible that the billions of chickens raised for meat or eggs are the most abused animals on the planet.

Cows and pigs face similar conditions. Dairy cows are stressed in ways similar to egg-laying chickens. Cows are continually impregnated, reducing their average life span, and thanks to the hormones, antibiotics, and other chemicals, dairy cows now produce ten times as much milk than they naturally would. These and other factors, such as the stress of confinement and continual mastitis infections, contribute to the decrease of dairy cows' average life span from twenty-five to five years.[12]

Of the one hundred million pigs raised each year, 97 percent of them are raised on factory farms and spend their entire lives so intensely confined that many cannot turn around. Well over a million pigs and cows die and hundreds of thousands of others are injured each year in transport from factory farm to slaughterhouses. There are countless accounts by slaughterhouse workers that many large animals die *during* the slaughter process, as opposed to the beginning. A typical pig slaughterhouse can kill as many as eleven hundred pigs per hour, making humane slaughter impossible.[13] Once we understand the process that produces our meat, milk, and eggs, the questions are, Are we raising animals or food machines? and, Can we bless this food?

It's not just the immediate concern for how we treat animals and produce food at the expense of the land and even our own bodies (including workers); these methods don't make long-term, overall sense. Decreasing biodiversity in the genetics of the plants and animals we eat puts at risk our long-term survival. As conditions change globally, the genetic variety in our foods gives us increased options as we adapt to the changes in our climate and terrain. Industrialized practices put our long-term health at risk as we consume foods that have been genetically modified, treated with chemicals, and injected with steroids and antibiotics. Agribusiness farming uses vast amounts of resources and creates excessive pollution of the planet that could cause widespread collapse or cost us trillions of dollars to repair—or both.

Our industrialized practices depicted in the film *Our Daily Bread* demonstrate the agribusiness's assault on biodiversity, what is in food, and the resource consumption and pollution produced in industrial food production. The documentary left Sarah thinking that at each step in the process there is a better way—better for the animals, of course, but also better for the health of people and for the environment of our planet. However, change in production of our food that would allow for a more ethical treatment of animals, for better environmental use of the planet and for improved health conditions of workers and consumers would indirectly decrease efficiency and profit—the goals of industrialized food production. It makes the most difference in what one thinks is "better." At seven and eight years old, "better" is not cold, foreign, and harmful industrialized practices.

...and There Was Enough

Fundamental fact: as a nation and as a world, we have enough food for everyone on this planet to eat a balanced and nutritious diet. So where did we go wrong in our own Garden of Agricultural Eden? The root cause of hunger and malnutrition is poverty, not quantity. In developing countries, one in six people and one in three children under age five are undernourished. As of 2005, 16,400 children worldwide died per day and thirty-five million Americans, mostly children, went hungry because of poverty. To change these facts and the fact that one in three people around the world suffers from vitamin A, iron, and iodine deficiencies would cost our world $24 billion per year to make well. Yet in 2005, Americans alone spent $42 billion to lose weight.[14] While one in six people is hungry, malnourished, and too poor to pay for good food, another one in six is overeating, overnourished, and paying to lose weight. We are out of balance, but it is not the amount of food in this world or how many mouths to feed in the world that is the problem. It is the system that produces our food, the rules that govern that system, and the money that pays for the system.

Remember, we have enough food to feed everyone on the planet. There is not a need to produce more food, and yet we spray millions of pounds of chemicals in vain on crops to increase production; 37 percent of the U.S. food supply is lost to pests today versus 31 percent in the 1940s, despite our use of synthetic pesticides today. We choose chemicals that harm our health to produce more crops to feed to animals packed tightly in spaces and to waste (the United States throws away $43 billion of food a year). It doesn't make sense. The only part that adds up is that this system produces the

> **Fundamental fact: as a nation and as a world, we have enough food for everyone on this planet to eat a balanced and nutritious diet. So where did we go wrong in our own Garden of Agricultural Eden? The root cause of hunger and malnutrition is poverty, not quantity.**

most money for the owners of the companies that control food in the short term. The lack of food is a distribution problem; wealth is in the hands of a few instead of the many as it was in the traditional, small farm system.

Eating Oil

Our present system of production and distribution of food has changed with this process, too, as we expect on a regular basis to eat foods not grown in our local communities. This method of production, distribution, and consumption is increasingly unsustainable. This food production and distribution system uses more fossil fuel than any other sector in the U.S. economy—19 percent. In 1940 we consumed 2.3 calories of food for every 1 calorie of fossil fuel that it took to get it there. Today it's 10 calories of fossil fuel to produce 1 calorie of supermarket food.

Since I love fresh vegetables, fruit, and fish but unlike Sarah live in a part of the country where they are available only a few short months per year if at all, I end up eating road-weary salads (and I can taste the difference when I eat more locally). The important thing is to be mindful of those choices. By using a website (www.indo.com/cgi-bin/dist), I estimated the miles that a fruit salad would have to travel to Minnesota. Here's what one salad might rack up in frequent flyer miles to get to my plate:

- Grapes from Chile—5,578 miles
- Cherries from Michigan—513 miles
- Mandarin oranges from China—7,000 miles
- Strawberries from California—1,562 miles
- Canned peaches from Michigan—513 miles
- Bananas from Peru—4,058 miles

Healthy for me, not always so healthy for the environment—or the fruit!

Bill McKibben said in an interview on *Speaking of Faith* that most of our food (and he lives in Vermont so he has the same issues as I do in Minnesota) comes on the average two thousand miles to our plate. That's quite a journey! He advocates for more local eating not only to reduce the fossil fuel energy but also to improve the quality of community. When we eat locally, we're more likely to encounter our neighbor, resulting in more relationships. Specifically McKibben advocates for shopping at farmer's markets rather than supermarkets because they create more community.

> The real reason that's so interesting that we like farmers' markets, I think, turns out to be they're different. Parasociologists followed shoppers first through the supermarket, then through the farmers' market. Everybody's been to the supermarket. You know how it works. You walk in, you fall into a light fluorescent trance. You visit the stations of the cross around the perimeter of the supermarket. You emerge with your items. That's it. When they followed people around the farmers' market, they were having, on average, 10 times as many conversations per visit.[15]

The result of less local farming coupled with other technologies has changed the way we eat, even within the last generation. Just as the changes in the environment have affected the diet of Kenya within a generation, as told in Wangari Maathai's story, our own food and nutrition have changed, too. People do not eat quite the same way in the United States as they did in the first half of the twentieth century as a result of large, military-industrial-complex farming prevalent in the United States today.

People cook less of their own food than they once did, throwing away more than they ever have. Many people don't know how to cook, or they maintain that they don't like to cook. Women of my generation or even my mother's felt that cooking was drudgery. Professional women who still work "two shifts," one at a workplace and the other when they get home, don't want to cook because there just isn't enough time in the day or night to do it all.

There was a whole cultural phenomenon in 1960 when Peg Bracken published her *I Hate to Cook Book,* which significantly influenced women who were at the cusp of the feminist movement into believing that cooking wasn't something worthwhile or valuable work, much less enjoyable. Cheap, common, convenient, canned, frozen, or boxed foods were the watchwords in Bracken's recipes. Some foods like tater tots and canned cream of mushroom soup with beans soon began to appear at church potlucks and in church cookbooks, forever changing the ecclesiastical fare, too! (When I go to church potlucks in the traditionally Scandinavian culture of Minnesota, one would assume that the Vikings ate mushroom soup and tater tots!)

Lately and slowly, cooking has taken on a more acceptable status in our society. As the economic downturn was occurring in the fall of 2008, I was talking to a young adult who is married and had one child at the time. For some reason we began to talk about cooking. He loves to cook and comes from an ethnic heritage that has unique foods and recipes. His mother, who married into the ethnic heritage, had learned all the recipes from her mother-in-law. Now he is learning them from his mother.

But he told me that his brothers don't know how to cook. In fact, one of them was struggling financially, and one reason was that he was accustomed to eating out all the time: a financial luxury that he could no longer sustain. We talked about how home-cooked food is also better for you—usually healthier with fewer calories. It costs less, and while it is more time-consuming, preparing as well as eating food is increasingly becoming a family activity that connects work and fun.

Furthermore, we tend to eat alone more than people did forty to fifty years ago. Then single people were more likely to live in extended family arrangements and less likely to eat day after day by themselves. The irony is that studies indicate that eating in community usually results in more time spent eating, but paradoxically less weight is gained because people are more satisfied in eating.[16]

A just society doesn't encourage highly processed foods full of salt, fat, and sugar to be significantly less expensive than healthy food. Poor families are forced to choose less healthy foods at the supermarket (if they have a supermarket in their community and don't have to rely on a high-priced convenience store) because they can fill more stomachs longer with less money.

Likewise, food donation centers end up giving out primarily packaged, processed, and generally unhealthy foods filled with salt, sugar, and fat. Packaged and processed food creates large profits for a handful of large, multinational corporations, thanks to specific commodity-based subsidies that overtax the American worker and pass on the costs (health and otherwise) to the poor, the planet, and the underrepresented.

We have increased yields, efficiency, and profits, but at what cost?

Who pays for the cheap foods that we eat? In what ways do the animals, field and slaughterhouse workers, and the health of consumers pay for what we eat and the cheap price we pay for food? How might we instead pay the price to feed the hungry of our world?

The current industrialized food system is unjust. It's unjust to farmers, to the poor in this country, to the animals we consume, and to the developing world. The industrialized system's goals to maximize efficiency to maximize profit come at a cost. This cost is paid for by poor people, people who suffer from food-related disease (such as type 2 diabetes), the animals, and the least among us worldwide.

Would Jesus *buy* food that was produced in this way? Would Jesus *bless* the food that comes from this production system?

WWJE?

Sarah keeps asking, "What would Jesus eat?" Multiplying the loaves and fish provided mercy at the time, but Jesus calls us to justice, too. Mercy mops up the problem of a broken pipe for the time being, but justice addresses what caused the broken pipe to begin with. When Jesus said that whatever we do to the least of these (Matthew 25:31-46) we do to him, I believe that it was for purposes of mercy *and* justice. People need food, water, a home, clothing, and a visit for the sick and imprisoned, but they also need for us to eliminate the causes of food scarcity, hydrological poverty, and labor and health-related injustices.

Performing acts of mercy is easier for us as Christians than performing acts of justice. Changing policy is among the most difficult acts to be informed about, to understand, to participate in, and to advocate for, but it is the most systemic and transforming action in order to eliminate poverty and hunger in the United States.

As a child, Sarah remembers her father explaining to her at the East Ohio Annual Conference of The United Methodist Church that a resolution had been brought forth to boycott Taco Bell as a way to send the message that the United Methodists of East Ohio were not supportive of Taco Bell's employment and treatment of their tomato farmers in Florida. "I was taken aback. I felt so proud," Sarah said. "My church was taking a stand for people in Florida who were not able to stand up for themselves. And we were doing it in a way in which even I, as a child, could participate." Sarah and her brothers were not going to go to Taco Bell.[17] A food rule came into existence in the Ehrman household.

Food Rules

Food rules existed from the very beginning of our Judeo-Christian traditions, and yet for some reason Christians today mostly believe that they should be and, practically speaking, are free of all food rules. As Christians, we can eat whatever we want, no matter how it is raised or prepared or whether it's healthy or blessed!

Throughout our salvation history, God has given us food rules. Food rules were given right away in the Garden of Eden. Later when the people were in the wilderness after leaving Egypt, they were hungry, and Moses was instructed to tell the people that God would provide for them—but food rules went along with the supply of manna and quail. They were to gather "enough for that day" (Exodus 16:4). Not too much and not too little, but enough for one's daily bread and meat. If they gathered too much, it rotted, and if they gathered too little, they still had enough (Exodus 16:18). God's provisions were enough, just right for what the people needed. Furthermore, they were to gather enough for the Sabbath.

The Law establishes food rules, specifying what to eat and what not to eat. Ellen Davis points out that Leviticus 11, which delineates clean and unclean food (the food rules for faithfulness to God), is exactly in the center of the Law;[18] food rules were central to obedience and faithfulness to God.

Jesus was accused of eating and drinking instead of fasting, but in the desert when tempted by the devil, he said no to the limitless, self-referential power that Satan was offering him. In essence, he was reversing the sin in Eden by his limitation or restriction on food. Early Christians vacillated about food rules because they believed that Gentiles were also welcome at the table. Food—or eating together—became metaphoric for the inclusion of the church.

Throughout Christianity, fasting has been a way of opening oneself to God. In effect it is a way that people have made a connection between food and faith. Yet for many modern Christians, the emphasis on fasting is usually more about losing weight than about drawing closer to God. Fasting means limiting or restricting what one eats, and it seems applicable to modern food rules that promote "just eating."

I wonder what kind of food rules Jesus would suggest for us today, especially based on "just eating"? "Just eating" is trying to eat in such a way that we care for the earth, our bodies, and our neighbors; it's a lot to ask of food! But it's also about expecting that our food is grown in such a way that earth can continue to sustain life for all and not just for some, now and in the future, in the United States and around the world.

> "Just eating" is trying to eat in such a way that we care for the earth, our bodies, and our neighbors.

The food rules from Leviticus aren't going to work in our modern, Christian context, but what will help us to live more healthfully and sustainably in our eating? I suggest Michael Pollan's rules for food that sidestep the temptation to eat according to the bathroom scales and more toward the scales of justice in our military-industrial complex:

The Omnivore's Solution: A New Way to Eat in the New Year

1. Don't eat anything your grandmother wouldn't recognize as food.
2. Avoid foods containing ingredients you can't pronounce.
3. Don't eat anything that won't eventually rot.
4. Avoid food products that carry health claims.
5. Shop the peripheries of the supermarket; stay out of the middle.
6. Better yet, buy food somewhere else: the farmer's market or CSA [community supported agriculture].
7. Pay more, eat less.
8. Eat a wide diversity of species.
9. Eat food from animals that eat grass.
10. Cook and, if you can, grow some of your own food.
11. Eat meals and eat them only at tables.
12. Eat deliberately, with other people whenever possible, and always with pleasure.[19]

These food rules offer personal and environmentally healthy habits that are consistent with the food rules of the Scriptures and a sustainable environment. How could churches participate in supporting people who are seeking to eat by such food rules? By hosting farmers' markets and CSAs? By sharing grass-fed beef or other local meats from a local farmer? By cooking and eating together more regularly?

Food rules sound alien to many of us, but a younger generation is coming to learn about the need for them. Sarah and her significant other, Chris, have explained to Chris's seven- and eight-year-old boys at dinner how high fructose corn syrup affects the planet and their bodies. These two boys care deeply about the planet and are willing to make tough choices to live by what they believe is right. They read labels on packaging now and ask if something has corn syrup. They take pride in choosing foods without this additive. Healthy eating has gone far beyond whether a child will choose an apple instead of a candy bar for a snack!

As Sarah learned more about the way the majority of food is raised, produced, and processed, she felt overwhelmed. And it wasn't just meat. It was fish that were overfished, genetically engineered, and farmed. It was genetically modified and heavily subsidized corn and soy. It was the pesticides, herbicides, working conditions, and fossil fuel that went into the process of getting produce from fifteen hundred miles away, on average, to her table. It was hard to know what was wrong with each food and whether alternatives she considered were really any better. The increased knowledge of the processes reinforced that she needed to change the way she ate, but it made her feel more helpless in determining just what to do.

Sarah worked at developing her own food rules: "I have been experimenting with and working toward taking steps—sometimes small steps—toward healthier, more environmentally sound, and ethical eating. I realized that it is not a set of hard and fast rules that makes for perfect eating conditions, but a continual restructuring of choices around food."

Years back, Sarah would have thought that if she had her own land with a chicken coop, a goat or two, an extensive year-round garden (she can do that in California), and fruit trees, she could achieve perfection. She has come to realize that even this dream misses the connection and community that come from "just eating" practices.

Sarah had an opportunity to tour a slaughterhouse recently. "I taught about factory farming and the slaughter of animals for years. I'd seen documentaries like *Fast Food Nation*. I use animal parts, fetal pigs from slaughtered sows, and full-size cats in the dissections I do with my anatomy students every year," she said. "While these prepared me for what I would see, nothing prepared me for the feeling I had during and after the tour.

"There were so many animals. They hung everywhere. I squeezed between the animals to see different stations in the process. It was unreal at times; somewhat fascinating in how different it was from anything I had ever seen as I saw even the insides of animals. While the tour was an odd combination of being fascinated and disturbed, after the tour I felt terrible. It was a haunting feeling. It was exactly as Harry Potter describes feeling after a run-in with the dementors. Again, it is not that I am against killing and eating animals. The number of animals was overwhelming, and the process was so unnatural.

"I've been interested in getting a cut of beef from a locally slaughtered steer, and now it seems that I will have the chance to do that as well as see it shot. I'm not excited about seeing it shot and I am nervous about it, but there is something in me that believes that if I am not truly accepting of the process, then maybe that meat has no place on my table.

"At the end of the day, I want to be able to bless the food at my table. I want to bless each step of the process that brought it there as well. Only then will I be comfortable inviting Jesus to my table."

These are some of Sarah's goals, or perhaps they could be called her food rules:

- to eat foods that have not been treated with chemicals,
- to eat food that is local (within 150 miles),
- to eat meat that is from small family farms and is sustainably raised and humanely slaughtered,
- to decrease my meat consumption,
- to eat less packaged food,
- and to grow and prepare more and more of the food I eat.

Sarah's ultimate goal is to be an old, old woman. She means that not in terms of age, but in terms of being like our grandmothers and their mothers were years before her: "Someday I would like to get all I eat from my garden, from farmers' markets, and from local produce markets. I'd like to make my own breads, pasta, refried beans, and cookies from bulk grains. I'd like to can tomatoes for sauce and make my own jams. I'd like to buy only foods that look exactly like what they are—whole foods that are not packaged, modified, or preserved in any way. Most of all, I would like to live within a food community—knowing who I buy food from, sharing what I know and the food I eat with as many people around me as possible, and supporting the health, spirits, environments around me. I'm hoping Aunt Sally is among them!"

On a minute scale, Sarah and others like her practice this farming in their own gardens. All gardeners monitor the weather to determine when to plant and water. They pay attention to browning and yellowing leaves and look around for bugs. Slowly they experiment and gauge the soil quality, adding their own compost, testing the limits of how tightly they can pack in the plants without losing quantity or quality per bed. Sarah refuses to use chemicals and synthetic fertilizers. Instead she encourages garden spiders, praying mantises, and beneficial pest control critters, and she has even considered a duck since they are known to be incredibly good at picking pests off plants. She uses her own compost pile and chooses to rotate in specific plants to replenish the soil with nutrients.

Hopeful signs include the fact that more and more people are finding ways to grow their own food, even in the cities and suburbs. A pot of basil or tomatoes on the deck, a small raised garden behind the house, and community gardens now appear throughout our country. When Michelle Obama dug up the south lawn of the White House to engage children (including her own) in the growing of food, she made a statement about the importance of healthy food: knowing where our food comes from, having a connection to our food, and working together in community.

An Inspiring Example

Community supported agriculture is a growing phenomenon with small farmers in relationship with their surrounding communities, including the urban and suburban dwellers. Churches and other community groups can reduce their carbon footprints by supporting them, sharing a bountiful box of produce each week from them. Anathoth

Community Garden in Cedar Grove, North Carolina, is an example of a rural community that addressed numerous problems of racism, poverty, and violence.

The Anathoth Community Garden had much of its motivation and direction from the Cedar Grove United Methodist Church, which many had viewed as the "rich white church." Following a 2004 shooting of a nearby store owner, the church was instrumental in calling for a prayer vigil. A member of the community was moved by the community coming together in prayer and decided that something could be done to help continue to heal the brokenness in the community and so gave five acres to the community. At the same time, the Cedar Grove church was trying to find a way to address poverty. The community garden grew out of the dream, raising food together for one another. In addition to a diversity of plant species in the garden, there's a diversity of humanity: Asians, Latinos, African and European Americans, and Christians and non-Christians come together to work the land, cook, and eat together.[20]

What if the acres of lawns we mow at our churches, homes, and communities were cultivated so that people could meet their neighbors; have healthy, fresh food to eat; and learn new skills for life? In local communities across the country, we could feed the masses!

Continuing the Journey—Stay in Love with God

So much of staying in love with God is centered in forgiveness and reconciliation. The way in which Christians in particular have ignored, neglected, and outright denied our relationship to care for the earth is in need of our repentance. To care for the earth is to ask God's forgiveness for the ways in which we as North Americans have harmed the earth. Some find the desert creeping or even sweeping across their lands, leaving them with less firewood and food. Others find the waters of the ocean overtaking their island homes, forcing them to relocate in other countries as refugees. We must also ask forgiveness from our brothers and sisters around the planet who suffer from our direct and indirect impact on their environments.

Staying in love with God also means doing justice.

Again, I'm reminded of Eugene Peterson's translation of the prophet Isaiah:

I'm sick of your religion, religion, religion,
    while you go right on sinning.
When you put on your next prayer-performance,
    I'll be looking the other way.
No matter how long or loud or often you pray,
    I'll not be listening.
And do you know why? Because you've been tearing
    people to pieces, and your hands are bloody.
Go home and wash up.
    Clean up your act.
Sweep your lives clean of your evildoings
    so I don't have to look at them any longer.
Say no to wrong.
    Learn to do good.
Work for justice.
    Help the down-and-out.
Stand up for the homeless.
    Go to bat for the defenseless. (Isaiah 1:14-17
THE MESSAGE)

The passage puts a fine point on this connection: all our religious practices aren't authentic unless we are working for justice, helping the down-and-out, and making this world a better place, not just for ourselves, but for our neighbors, near and far, now and in the future.

A Commitment

Take steps toward "just eating" in your daily life. If you can, participate in Communion, and be sure to say grace for the food you enjoy this week.

EPILOGUE

Say no to wrong.
Learn to do good.
Work for justice.
Help the down-and-out.
Stand up for the homeless.
Go to bat for the defenseless.
—*Isaiah 1:17* THE MESSAGE

It is our hope that this book will help all of us as Christians make the connections with what Jesus has taught us in his parables with the practices that care for God's earth. How we live on earth—how we "Work for justice. / Help the down-and-out. / Stand up for the homeless./ Go to bat for the defenseless," as the prophet Isaiah says—are practices that God desires from people who seek to be in relationship with God. We can attend seminars about the environment and we can make all kinds of statements, but we need to practice the ways of caring for the earth and the people of the earth as a sign of loving God.

Doing no harm, learning to do good, and staying in love with God are a repeating cycle. As we seek to do no harm, learn about and do good, and experience a closer relationship with God, we are encouraged to go to the next level of doing no harm, learning to do good, and again find ourselves being in closer relationship with God. And the cycle goes on.

We must bring our whole selves—minds, bodies, spirits, communities, and wills—to live as Jesus taught us. We can't do it by ourselves; we need one another. We call on communities of faith to come together in small groups and as congregations to support and encourage one another as they do no harm, do good, and stay in love with God in regard to caring for the earth.

NOTES

Introduction: The Genesis
1. Genesis 1:1–2:2a is a later account, believed to be written during the time of the exile of Israel (sixth century B.C.E). Genesis 2:2a-25 is an earlier account, believed to be written during the tenth century B.C.E.

Chapter 1: Our Three Temptations
1. Krista Tippett with Bill McKibben, "The Moral Math of Climate Change," *Speaking of Faith,* December 10, 2009, http://speaking offaith.publicradio.org/programs/2009moral-math/transcript.shtml.
2. http://www.globio.org/glossopedia/article.aspx?art_id=6#.
3. http://rainforests.mongabay.com/amazon/rainforest_ecology.html.
4. http://www.globio.org/glossopedia/article.aspx?art_id=6#.
5. Tyler G. Miller, *Living in the Environment,* 15th ed. (Belmont, Calif.: Brooks/Cole, 2007), 117.
6. http://www.globio.org/glossopedia/article.aspx?art_id=6#.
7. Miller, *Living in the Environment,* 117.
8. Ibid., 118.
9. http://rainforests.mongabay.com/amazon/rainforest_ecology.html.
10. http://www.elephantjournal.com/2010/06/every-second-2-football-fields-worth-of-rainforest-are-lost/.
11. Miller, *Living in the Environment,* 119.
12. http://environment.about.com/od/healthenvironment/a/rain forest_drug.htm.
13. David A. Wilkinson, "Lesson 2: Friends or Foes? The Story of a Complex Relationship," tracks 3 and 4 on *Religion and Science: Pathways to Truth,* www.WesleyMinistryNetwork.com.
14. UMNS commentary by Rev. Tina Carter, July 16, 2010, http://www.umc.org/site/apps/nlnet/content3.aspx?c=lwL4KnN1LtH &b=5259669&ct=8532087&tr=y&auid=6645810.
15. Ellen Davis, *Scripture, Culture, and Agriculture* (New York: Cambridge University Press, 2009), 55.

16. See Davis's interpretations of how the Law provides for the sustainability of the land in her book *Scripture, Culture, and Agriculture*. (You'll have a whole new appreciation for the books of the Law!)
17. *Webster's New World Dictionary* (New York: World Publishing, 1972), 1564.
18. Davis, *Scripture, Culture, and Agriculture*, 55.
19. Ibid., emphasis added.
20. "Preface to 1739 Hymns and Sacred Poems," *The Works of John Wesley*, Jackson Edition, volume 14 (1831), 321.
21. Krista Tippett, "Planting the Future," *Speaking of Faith*, April 30, 2009, http://speakingoffaith.publicradio.org/programs/2009/plant ingthefuture/.
22. Ibid.
23. Ibid.
24. Wangari Maathai, *Unbowed* (New York: Random House, 2007), 179–80.
25. John Wesley's words were "attending upon all the ordinances of God." See *The Book of Discipline of The United Methodist Church* (Nashville: The United Methodist Publishing House, 2008), 74.
26. Rueben P. Job, *Three Simple Rules* (Nashville: Abingdon Press, 2007), 11.
27. Ibid.
28. Ibid.,11–12.
29. Ibid., 16.

Chapter 2: Consider the Earth
1. "The Historical Roots of Our Ecologic Crisis," *Science* 155, no. 3767 (March 10, 1967): 1203.
2. The World Health Organization estimates that 80 percent of the world's people rely on medicines derived from plants in the rainforest, and cancer drugs derived from chemicals found in the tropical rainforest save thirty thousand lives and provide $350 billion in economic benefits. Tyler G. Miller, *Living in the Environment*, 15th ed. (Belmont, Calif.: Brooks/Cole, 2007), 205.
3. E. O. Wilson, *The Future of Life* (New York: Vintage Books, 2002), 106.
4. Brendan Kennelly, "Whenever That Happened," in *Poems to Live By in Troubling Times*, ed. Joan Murray (Boston: Beacon Press, 2006), 41.

5. Ibid.

6. Bill McKibben, "Consuming Nature," in *The Bill McKibben Reader: Pieces from an Active Life* (New York: Henry Holt, 2008), 20.

7. Ibid.

8. Hanna Rosen, "Did Christianity Cause the Crash?" *Atlantic,* December 2009, http://www.theatlantic.com/doc/print/200912/rosin-prosperity-gospel.

9. See *The Book of Discipline of The United Methodist Church* (Nashville: The United Methodist Publishing House, 2008), 73.

Chapter 3: The Love of Stuff

1. Leona Dueck Penner, "Too Much for One Canoe," *MCC Women's Concerns Report*, May-June 1991, 4–5. Based on a true story.

2. Eugene H. Peterson, *Tell It Slant: A Conversation on the Language of Jesus in His Stories and Prayers* (Grand Rapids: Eerdmans, 2008), 59.

3. Ibid., 62.

4. Adam Hamilton, *Enough: Discovering Joy through Simplicity and Generosity* (Nashville: Abingdon Press, 2009), 21.

5. Bill McKibben, "Hot and Bothered: Facing Up to Global Warming," *Christian Century* (July 11, 2006): 29, 31.

6. Bill McKibben, "Meltdown: Running Out of Time on Global Warming," *Christian Century* (February 20, 2007): 25.

7. *The Story of Stuff,* film by Annie Leonard (Free Range Studios, 2007), http://www.storyofstuff.org.

8. Minerals such as sand, aluminum, copper, platinum, steel (a combination of manganese, copper, chromium, and iron), limestone, gold, and many others; water; trees; fossil fuels such as coal, oil, and natural gas; and even animal and plant life are natural resources involved in making "stuff."

9. *The Story of Stuff.*

10. Ibid.

11. Ibid.

12. Ibid.

13. Ibid.

14. Rueben P. Job, *Three Simple Rules* (Nashville: Abingdon Press, 2007), 58.

Chapter 4: Creating Hell All around Us

1. Nicholas D. Kristof, "Where Sweatshops Are a Dream," *New York Times*, January 15, 2009.
2. Tyler G. Miller, *Living in the Environment,* 15th ed. (Belmont, Calif.: Brooks/Cole, 2007), 521.
3. http://www.oberlin.edu/recycle/facts.html#styrofoam.
4. Miller, *Living in the Environment,* 531.
5. Ibid., 532.
6. *Trashed: This Is the Story of Garbage...American Style,* film (OXI Productions, 2007), www.trashedmovie.com/.
7. Ibid.
8. Ibid.
9. http://www.cbsnews.com/stories/2008/11/06/60minutes/main 4579229.shtml.
10. http://www.newsvine.com/_news/2007/11/18/1106074-amer ica-ships-electronic-waste-overseas.
11. http://www.pbs.org/frontlineworld/stories/ghana804/video/video_index.html.
12. http://www.basel.int/ratif/convention.htm.
13. The documentary *Recycled Life,* a film by Leslie Iwerks and Mike Glad (2006), tells the story of the people living in the largest garbage dump in Guatemala. Go to http://www.recycledlifedoc.com.
14. Bill McKibben, "Meltdown: Running Out of Time on Global Warming," *Christian Century* (February 20, 2007): 24.
15. "Cabinet Makes Splash with Underwater Meeting," msnbc.com, http://www.msnbc.msn.com/id/33354627/print/1/displaymode/1098/.
16. See a video of the Smokey Mountain Church's school for children: http://new.gbgm-umc.org/about/us/mcr/?search=garbagedumps&C=5012&I=15070.
17. Kathleen LaCamera, *Ministry to the Least of These,* Mission Papers 2008, General Board of Global Ministries. See Kathleen La-Camera's full report: http://new.gbgm-umc.org/news/themes/gc/resources/?search=garbage dumps&C=5305&I=16956.
18. Ibid.
19. "Mottainai! Saving Energy as Cultural Value," posted by Rob Schmitz, filed under Economics, Energy, International, Technology, October 11, 2009, http://blogs.kqed.org/climatewatch/2009/10/11/mottainai-saving-energy-as-cultural-value/.

20. For further discussion, see how one study has revealed how the U.S. population views the influence of humanity on the environment; "More Americans 'Dismissive' and Fewer 'Alarmed' About Global Warming," Yale University (February 23, 2010). A copy of the report on which the study is based is available online at http://environment.yale.edu/climate.

21. *The Book of Discipline of The United Methodist Church* (Nashville: The United Methodist Publishing House, 2008), 73.

Chapter 5: Take It to the Water

1. Wendell Berry, "God and Country," *What Are People For?* (New York: North Point Press, 1990), 98.

2. Emily Wax, "In Drought-choked Somalia, 'Thirst Forces Men to This Horror of War,' " *Star Tribune*, April 15, 2006, A1.

3. Ibid., A5.

4. Tyler G. Miller, *Living in the Environment*, 15th ed. (Belmont, Calif.: Brooks/Cole, 2007), 310.

5. Ibid., 306.

6. Ibid., 311.

7. *Enough*, no. 2 in a series on climate change, Church World Service, p. 2.

8. Nicholas D. Kristof and Sheryl WuDunn, *Half the Sky: Turning Oppression into Opportunity for Women Worldwide* (New York: Knopf, 2009), 169.

9. David Davies, "Hearts Drenched with Love," in *The Upper Room Disciplines, 2008* (Nashville: Upper Room Books, 2008), 66.

10. Amy-Jill Levine, *The Misunderstood Jew: The Church and the Scandal of the Jewish Jesus* (San Francisco: HarperSanFrancisco, 2006), 135.

11. Miller, *Living in the Environment*, 305.

12. http://www.oikoumene.org/news/news-management/eng/a/article/1634/taking-water-to-the-jorda-2.html.

13. "Pollution Threatens Revered Jordan River," *U.S. Water News Online,* November 2005, http://www.uswaternews.com/archives/arcglobal/5pollthre11.html.

14. Miller, *Living in the Environment*, 305.

15. Ibid., 311.

16. *Blue Gold: World Water Wars*, film by Sam Bozzo (Purple Turtle Films, 2010).

17. Ibid.
18. Ibid.
19. Ibid.
20. Charles Fishman, "Message in a Bottle," *Fast Company*, December 19, 2007, http://www.fastcompany.com/magazine/117/features-message-in-a-bottle.html, 4.
21. Ibid., 2.
22. Ibid., 7.
23. Ibid.
24. Ibid., 2.
25. Ibid., 11.

Chapter 6: Bless This Food!
1. "Table for Six Billion, Please!" is the international sister restaurant project in which sister relationships are formed between the White Dog Café and restaurants in countries where there is poor dialogue with the United States, http://www.whitedog.com/int_sis.html.
2. Ellen Davis, *Scripture, Culture, and Agriculture* (New York: Cambridge University Press, 2009), 164.
3. Tyler G. Miller, *Living in the Environment*, 15th ed. (Belmont, Calif.: Brooks/Cole, 2007), 276
4. Ibid.
5. Ibid., 274.
6. *Our Daily Bread*, film by Nikolaus Geyrhalter (Icarus Films, 2005).
7. It's important for the reader to understand that the environmental information and science given in this book are the standard information and science given in classrooms across the United States today. As younger generations learn about the way in which the earth is being treated, even by their own habits, they will demand changes in business, industry, options for packaging and recycling, housing, and so on.
8. http://www.goveg.com/factoryFarming_chickens.asp.
9. http://www.idausa.org/facts/factoryfarmfacts.html.
10. http://www.goveg.com/factoryFarming_chickens.asp.
11. Ibid.
12. http://www.goveg.com/factoryFarming_cows.asp.
13. http://www.goveg.com/factoryFarming_pigs.asp.
14. Miller, *Living in the Environment*, 274.

15. Bill McKibben, "The Moral Math of Climate Change," *Speaking of Faith*, December 10, 2009, http://being.publicradio.org/programs/2009/moral-math/transcript.shtml.

16. Tara Parker-Pope, "Instead of Eating to Diet, They're Eating to Enjoy," *New York Times*, September 17, 2008.

17. The boycott began in 2001 across the church in support of farm workers and labor conditions and ended following a General Conference endorsement in September 2004, http://archives.umc.org/interior.asp?ptid=2&mid=5685.

18. Davis, *Scripture, Culture, and Agriculture*, 95.

19. From an advertisement in the *New York Times*, January 3, 2008, B12. Based on Pollan's *In Defense of Food: An Eater's Manifesto* (New York: Penguin Press, 2008).

20. Davis, *Scripture, Culture, and Agriculture*, 118.

CPSIA information can be obtained at www.ICGtesting.com
Printed in the USA
LVOW010021190213

320637LV00001B/2/P

9 781426 710377